THE Fender STRATOCASTER

by
A.R. DUCHOSSOIR

Special Foreword by
ERIC CLAPTON

HAL•LEONARD®

Published by Hal Leonard Corporation
7777 West Bluemound Road, P.O. Box 13819, Milwaukee, WI 53213 USA
REVISED EDITION

A FEW WORDS FROM
ERIC CLAPTON
ABOUT THE STRATOCASTER...

Everyone has a different reason for picking up and playing the guitar — For some it is an absolute compulsion to express and display their God given gift, for others it is simply a desire to emulate their heroes. For myself, it was, and still is, a combination of both. In the pursuit of this sometimes impossible quest, I have tried just about every guitar that has ever been made, and without fail I always come back to the 'stratocaster,' it's just like going home again. It is mean and yet comfortable, crude and yet pure. It's about as close to being perfect as any electric guitar can be — Take my advice, pick one up, plug it in, and play, I think you will see what I mean —

Yours Truly —

Eric Clapton
87

ACKNOWLEDGEMENTS

The author wishes to extend his thanks to the following people for their contribution to this book.

Patrice BASTIEN, Bill BLACKBURN, Gorge BLANDA, Klaus BLASQUIZ, Bruce BOLEN, Mike CAROFF, Bill CARSON, Eric CLAPTON, Ken COLLINS, Jim CRUICKSHANK, Vic Da PRA, Lee DICKSON, Didier DODEMAN, Ralph ESPOSITO, Steve EVANS, Yves FARGE, the FENDER CUSTOM SHOP, Gérard FERAUD, Brian FISCHER, George FULLERTON, Uncle Lou GATANAS, Dany GIORGETTI, Scott GRANT, Jeff GRAY, George GRUHN, John GRUNDER, Larry HENRICKSON, John HILL, Susan LANDAU, Philip LANG, Perry MARGOULEFF, Jacques MAZZOLENI, Jean Claude MEINIAN, John PAGE, John PEDEN, Ricardo RODRIGUEZ, Alan ROGAN, Bill SCHULTZ, Dan SMITH, Richard SMITH, Steve SOEST, John SPRUNG, Michael STEVENS, Freddie TAVARES, Malcolm TUTE, Clay WADE & James WERNER.

THE Fender® STRATOCASTER

CONTENTS

THE INVENTION OF THE STRATOCASTER

There have been many books and articles published about the Stratocaster – including the author's previous edition of this book – , but the true origins of this "guitare extraordinaire" are still open to some controversy. More is known today about early FENDER history, yet the recollections of the key individuals involved in its development do not always perfectly match. This is hardly surprising since it involves recalling events which took place some 40 years ago, often without the help of supportive documentation. Tracking down the actual beginnings of the Stratocaster is rather like an investigation... after hearing witnesses, crosschecking stories, finding out facts and reassessing past statements, one eventually comes up with a personal belief intended to set the record as straight as possible.

THE BIRTH OF A LEGEND

The Stratocaster was born in the early 1950's in Southern California, and more precisely in Fullerton, near Los Angeles, hometown of the FENDER MUSICAL INSTRUMENT Co. By all accounts, at least 3 individuals were instrumental to different degrees in the advent of the guitar : LEO FENDER, of course, FREDDIE TAVARES and BILL CARSON. Other people, such as DONALD RANDALL, GEORGE FULLERTON and REX GALLEON may have also shared some input before the Stratocaster made it to the production line in 1954.

One of the major discrepancies identified to this day in the origins of the Stratocaster concerns the actual years of its development. According to Leo Fender, the project goes back to the very early 1950's : **"We started to work on the Stratocaster around 1951 and the reason was we needed a new guitar with a vibrato on it in response to Bigsby's competition !"** (1). In another statement, Leo Fender went on to specify : **"It was mostly before Freddie [Tavares] came to work. It'd be around '51. We had the neck and body designed, and the pickups. I remember because, it was done before we moved from Pomona Street over to Valencia. I had most of the materials tooled and the parts in stock"** (2). It should be noted that the move to 122 Pomona Street only took place in 1953 and it was actually made public in June 1953 with the announcement of the formation of FENDER SALES Inc. Anyway, although the Stratocaster made its official debut in Spring 1954, Leo Fender predates its initial development back to 1951, probably in the latter part of the year after the introduction of the Precision Bass. Mr. Fender also mentioned on various occasions that he started the whole project shortly before he met Bill Carson, who later became his favourite 'guinea pig' to fieldtest the Stratocaster prototype.

Such statements are not fully corroborated by Freddie Tavares, who was hired by Leo Fender in early 1953 to assist him in the "lab", where new Fender products were then devised : **"I met Leo Fender about March of 1953. I was playing [steel guitar] in a club and he was introduced to me by a musician whose name was Noel Boggs. Noel told me Leo was looking for someone to work for him... The first real project that I had was to put the Stratocaster on drawing board. It was about April or May 1953 and Leo said we need a new guitar and I said how far apart are the strings at the nut, how far the bridge. I got those parameters and I said what's the scale and then I knew where the strings are and we started from there..."** (3). According to Freddie, the Stratocaster did not begin to take shape until he joined the Company in early 1953. Therefore, it could hardly have existed then in a pre-production stage, as implied by Leo Fender. Bill Carson was a country and western guitar player in the Eddy Kirk Band, when he first met Leo Fender in late 1951. He does not quite agree either with Mr Fender's agenda when he says : **"In 1952, Leo and I started talking about it [the Stratocaster], but we didn't really get anything done until early 1953 as I remember it"** (4). So, who has the better memory ?

Another important discrepancy relates to what prompted the advent of the Stratocaster. There is no doubt that Leo Fender wanted a "new guitar", be it to simply add a model to his limited range of Electric Spanish guitars, or to come up with an instrument clearly superior to the Telecaster and fitted with a vibrato tailpiece to satisfy the musical trends of the period. Both options were certainly supported by Don Randall, who was general manager of the RADIO & TELEVISION EQUIPMENT Co., then exclusive distributor of all Fender products (NB : FENDER SALES Inc. took over distribution as of June 1, 1953). According to Bill Carson, however, the Stratocaster was initially meant to be his "own custom-made guitar", built by Leo Fender to suit his professional requirements: **"I would say that 95% of the odd ideas in the original Strat were my ideas, but I couldn't put it together. I didn't have any engineering background or experience and all I could contribute was ideas... It [the original prototype] wasn't really intended, in my judgement, to ever be a commercially produced guitar. I believe the more he [Leo Fender] talked with me and then probably confirmed my ideas with a few other players around, that's when he made the decision that it could be a production guitar"** (5). Based on that assumption, Bill Carson was later billed by CBS/FENDER as "the man for whom the Stratocaster was designed" when the Anniversary Stratocaster was introduced in 1979. Beyond the controversy, one fact does seem to emerge: Leo Fender always welcomed the suggestions of the working musicians and he was keen to maintain a close relationship with them in order to improve his products. As outlined by Freddie Tavares: **"One of the reasons for Leo's success was that all the musicians knew that they were welcome in our lab. They could come out there and talk to us directly. Everybody knew they could get to Leo"** (6). Bill Carson acknowledges the fact and adds: **"Leo had a really uncanny ability to take what you were telling him and interpret the needs of that as a player. He didn't play guitar, he didn't think or hear in terms of a player, so he relied heavily on players who had good relative pitch"** (7).

In the light of fairly contradictory statements, it may appear kind of rash to give preference to one version and one course of events. But, 3 basic questions need to be answered : who did invent the Stratocaster ? How did it happen ? When did it take place ?

Way back in 1951 or 1952, Leo Fender was perhaps thinking of adding a companion to the straightforward Telecaster and Esquire guitars. He may well have given some thought to it or even roughly sketched some of the details likely to produce a "superior" instrument. His frequent meetings with working musicians such as Bill Carson probably confirmed then the need for an improved guitar. Eventually, the project of a "new" Fender guitar probably merged with the Carson request at some point in time, and it evolved into one instrument, later known as the Stratocaster.

It appears sensible to consider that Bill Carson certainly provided some ideas from a player's point of view, while Freddie Tavares definitely contributed to the design from a more technical point of view. Now, at the end of the day, there is no doubt that the new model was actually masterminded by Leo Fender himself. Freddie Tavares freely admits it : **"Leo wanted a better guitar, more improved, more versatile which he did get ! I put the lines on, but everything was under his thumb... so eventually it was all done to his satisfaction"** (8). With regard to time frame, it is the author's opinion that Mr Fender's memory may not be the most dependable one, when it comes to recalling his moments of genius in the 1950's. If one takes into account what happened at Fender over 1951 and 1952 – i.e. the introduction of the Precision Bass and the Stringmaster steel guitars, not to mention a growing activity in the field of amplifiers – it would seem unlikely that the actual design of the new model indeed began as early as Leo Fender is prone to remember. In spite of what he mentioned in various interviews, the development of the Stratocaster probably took place in 1953, as confirmed by Freddie

Mr LEO FENDER
at the punch press in 1954
(courtesy Forrest White/
Richard Smith)

A mid-50's picture of BILL CARSON
with his Cimarron red Stratocaster (courtesy Bill Carson)

FREDDIE TAVARES,
the man whose "French curves"
helped shape a legend
(courtesy Fender Musical Instruments)

Tavares : **"The design [of the Stratocaster] started in April or May of 1953 and it took less than a year"** (9). In fact, it could have happened quicker, if it were not for the vibrato tailpiece which required around six months to be perfected. This is certainly why Leo Fender said "materials were tooled and the parts in stock" with reference to the move from Pomona Street to East Valencia Street in mid-1953.

At any rate, even though he did not design the Stratocaster all by himself, Leo Fender, a man of plain appearance who could not play the guitar, made it become a reality. And to this day very few people have generated such a lasting impact on the music industry !

THE CONCEPTS BEHIND THE STRATOCASTER

In Spring 1954, when the Stratocaster was revealed to a bewildered music world just about to enter the rock 'n' roll era, it was offering several innovative, if not revolutionary, features. Its most radical appointments at the time were the novel "Synchronized Tremolo" system (NB: Fender used the word "tremolo" as a synonym for vibrato), and the "Comfort Contour Body". The new model could also boast a few other "Fender firsts", such as a fully adjustable bridge with 6 individual saddles, 3 pickups with staggered polepieces and a top-mounted plug receptacle. In spite of a greater sophistication in design than the Telecaster, the Stratocaster equally bore testimony to the Leo Fender philosophy, whereby instruments are meant for the working musicians. Freddie Tavares is keen to stress this concept: **"Leo Fender's attitude was: make it practical, as practical as possible, and as simple as possible...Leo was always that way, do it simpler and easier to service. Make it easy to fix"** (10). In this respect, Leo himself once said in an interview: **"I had so many years of experience with work on radios and electronics gear, and my main interest was in the utility aspects of an item. That was the main thing, appearance came next"** (11). The Stratocaster thus retained the basic structure of the previous Fender solid bodies, namely an ash body with a detachable one-piece maple neck (no separate fretboard), featuring an asymmetric peghead and a straight string pull on the tuners. The pickups assembly was affixed to a single plate, mounted on top of a routed body, so that every component could be easily removed and serviced if necessary. Leo Fender always made sure his products were practical and functional. He never relied on sheer theory or any kind of "blue sky" technology...just trial and error and experience to make better instruments. With regard to the Stratocaster, Freddie Tavares recalls: **"There was nothing special or theoretical about that design. It was just hit or miss, trial and error! The thing was that, loosely speaking, it couldn't have been another design the way we felt. It practically did itself out of utility. Everything we did, you might say we did empirically...all trails and errors"** (12).

The "Synchronized Tremolo"

As suggested by the first advertising campaign run in April 1954 by FENDER SALES Inc., the Synchronized Tremolo emerged as the most potent innovation on the Stratocaster. In the early 1950's, the Bigsby vibrato unit was enjoying a growing popularity, especially among those playing country & western music styles. The wham of the Memphis man or the Hendrix blazing attacks were not yet the name of the game, but in those days the vibrato effects "à la" steel guitar were widely appreciated. Bill Carson explains it : **"The value of a vibrato in those days was that steel guitar played a large part in country and western swing bands. When I was doing studio sessions with a foot control that Leo made me, I could use a vibrato and do steel guitar things and I would sometimes get paid double for the session. That was the reason why I wanted a vibrato !"** (13). The Fender sales force certainly did outline the desirability of such a device, and Freddie Tavares remembers quite bluntly : **"We didn't invent the tremolo thing. It had been used on many other instruments, but we wanted it because it seemed to be very saleable !"** (14). The needs of players like Bill Carson, combined with the requirements of the sales force, logically brought the vibrato tailpiece to the drawing board. The main problem in those days was that the vibratos available on the market

would not always come back to pitch, thus creating tuning difficulties. Therefore, the challenge facing Leo Fender was to devise a vibrato which would stay in tune.

The first vibrato designed by Leo Fender was, by all accounts, fairly similar to the unit later installed on the Jazzmaster guitar released in June 1958. It allowed some string length between the bridge and the tailpiece, where the strings were anchored. This early version was fitted with individual roller bearings, meant to facilitate return to pitch, but in fact they were damping the string sustain because of too much lateral vibration. It would also appear that the steel rod used as a tailpiece, did not anchor the strings firmly enough and their energy was dissipating to the detriment of tone and sustain. Leo Fender vividly remembers this troublesome design : **"We had problems with our first vibrato. It wouldn't sustain a tone... so we had to junk the whole thing and completely retool. It cost us about $ 5 000 in labour and machinery !"** (15). Bill Carson, who was then fieldtesting the prototype, suggested at first that the lack of sustain originated in the pickups, but this option was promptly discarded by Leo Fender : **"Bill thought it was the pickups, but it wasn't. They had no problems, but we had to completely retool the vibrato action. We had these little rollers on the bridge and they allowed lateral vibration. With a string, you can't have vibration in any direction at the bridge, it's got to be as solid as the Rock of Gibraltar !"** (16). Return to pitch was apparently OK, so the problem with tone and sustain was not deemed then to be that critical. This is probably why Leo Fender started to tool up at the factory in order to produce his first vibrato. When the problem crystallized, he tried to sort it out, no doubt convinced he could succeed in doing so. Freddie Tavares recalls with admiration : **"Leo Fender seemed to be able to solve any problem just by sitting there and thinking his head off... he was marvellous !"** (17). Leo Fender spent several months on his first vibrato, but he finally gave up in the latter part of 1953, so that the release of the new guitar would not be postponed any further, Freddie Tavares sums up the whole story when he says : **"When we made that vibrato device, everything was fine except the strings wouldn't sustain. There wasn't any inertia bar, just not enough weight... so we finally realized that the strings could not do their best job if they were loosely mounted, I mean not firmly mounted. That was the final thing. It took us almost 6 months - well, we had other things to do in the Company — to solve that problem !"** (18).

On the second version of the vibrato, Leo Fender took advantage of the principle of gram scales, which use a knife-edge, as a fulcrum. In other words, the vibrato mechanism was built INTO the bridge section and not set apart. His rationale was that the strings should no longer move across the bridge, but that the bridge itself should pivot on a knife-edge fulcrum point. The bridge base-plate was thus beveled to form a fulcrum ridge and secured to the body with 6 long hardened screws, one in front of each saddle. The "inertia bar" referred to by Freddie Tavares was secured to the outer side of the bridge base-plate and each string was firmly anchored through the vertical bores drilled into the bar. Return to pitch was accomplished by connecting 5 tension springs to the lower extremity of the inertia bar and hooking them onto the back of the body, in a recess routed towards the neck. With such a set-up, the 5 springs were adequately mounted in parallel to the strings to provide a perfect countertension to their pull. The countertension could, if necessary, be adjusted either by moving the 2 screws driven into the body to hold the spring plate, or by simply removing 1 or 2 of the 5 springs. This clever system would allow a good return to pitch, without killing sustain.

The (second issue) Synchronized Tremolo was finalized in the latter part of 1953 and within a year, on August 30, 1954, Leo Fender filed a patent for a "Tremolo device for stringed instruments". The patent was granted on April 10, 1956 and registered under the N° 2, 741, 146. It was "safer" to patent such a novel feature, because as George Fullerton, then factory production Foreman at FENDER, declares ; **"Patents prevent people from copying too quickly and this is a big thing in the music business Practically everything is copied overnight by somebody... it's not fair !"** (19). The wording clearly sums up the purpose of the invention of Clarence Leo Fender.

"The objects of my invention are :
FIRST, to provide a tremolo device which is particularly adapted for use on guitars... played in such a manner that one hand is the region of the bridge, there being a tremolo control arm so arranged as to fit within the palm of the player's hand.
SECOND, to provide a tremolo device which is incorporated in a novel

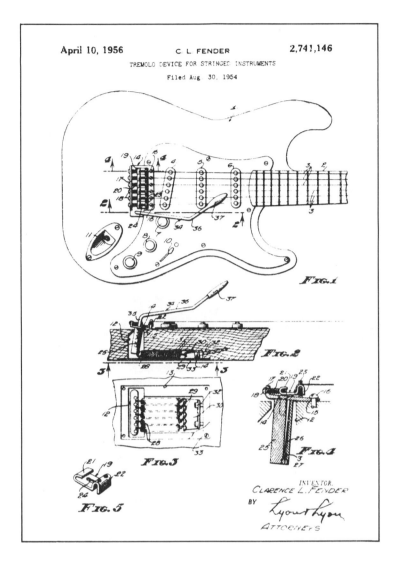

April 10, 1956   C. L. FENDER   2,741,146

TREMOLO DEVICE FOR STRINGED INSTRUMENTS

Filed Aug. 30, 1954

again, rooted in practicality. Despite the moderate thickness (i.e. 1.750") of the Telecaster, some players complained about its squared-off body, which was hurting them in the rib cage. Bill Carson says that he specifically talked to Mr Fender about this problem and he claims that he pretty much hammered the idea of a "contoured body" out of Leo : **"The thing I didn't like about the Telecaster was the discomfort of it, because I was doing a lot of studio work at the time on the West Coast and sitting down its square edges really dug into my rib. It [the Telecaster] didn't fit well and one of the things Leo got tired of hearing was that a guitar ought to fit you like a good shirt does !"** (20). Bill's claim is somewhat confirmed by Freddie Tavares, who declares : **"I'm not sure, but I think Leo got the idea of the contoured shape from Bill Carson"** (21). Leo Fender, howewer, gives credit to a local entertainer, by the name of Rex Galleon, for the relief made on the back of the instrument as well as the chamfer under the armrest : **"We'd shown this instrument to Rex Galleon before Bill came out, and it was Rex who was kind of responsible for the cutaway in the back and on the corner of the front face too, that was his suggestion"** (22). In the face of contradictory statements, the following rationale could be a possibility. Bill Carson admits that at first Leo Fender responded kind of negatively to his initial request to dress away the guitar body, because he felt it was too far-fetched. Bill also remembers that during the development of the Stratocaster, he had to leave California for a while to go and work in Canada. While Bill was away, Rex Galleon could have renewed or confirmed his wish to have a chamfered body shape and Leo would only recall this "second" request (?). Now, it also could be said that whoever asked first, Mr Fender may not have considered the request as a worthwile proposition until he had received the same request from other players. Freddie Tavares remembers that : **"Leo had a knack of thinking slowly and consecutively... no flashes of genius, but a merciless, unstoppable slow degree of thinking"** (23).

At any rate, when Leo Fender became convinced of the utility aspect of the contoured body, he simply began experimenting with it to define the right elements of comfort. Bill Carson testifies: **"I went one morning, this was early '53 as I remember, and Leo had sawed out 4 or 5 bodies for the relief, to see which one of those bodies did the job for me"** (24). It was soon realized that the relief would impact upon the overall shape of the instrument. Bill Carson recalls the progress then made on his "custom" guitar: **"The thing didn't balance. It looked somewhat like a Telecaster body in the beginning and so we started to lengthen that horn on top until it would balance. I think it was Freddie's suggestion that we extended the bottom horn to give it a little symmetry there and balance"** (25). In the process, the shape of the breadboard model gradually began to look like a downsized Precision Bass (NB: introduced in 1951). Was it exclusively achieved out of empirical research? Did Leo (and Freddie) more or less have in mind the idea to give a guitar mate to the P. Bass? Whatever the answer, there is no doubt that the final shape of the Stratocaster was formed out of utility, yet it has clearly become one of the most popular ever in terms of sheer aesthetic appeal. Many players indeed have picked up the Stratocaster on the face of its modernistic and flashy sculptured shape, before realizing how functional and enduring it is. The "Comfort Contour Body", first devised for the Stratocaster, later became a standard appointment on all the top range Fender instruments and it was thus fitted to the P. Bass by 1954. Oddly enough, Leo Fender did not immediately patent this novel structural feature. It was done with the advent of the Jazzmaster and the patent for the "Contour Body" (and the beveled "Off-Waist" design of the J. Master) was filed on January 13, 1958 and eventually granted on November 22, 1960.

bridge structure so arranged as to have limited pivotal movement, in order that the tension applied to the strings of the instrument may be readily varied to produce a tremolo effect.
THIRD, to provide in a tremolo device a novel sectional bridge so arranged that the effective operating length of each string and its height may be individually adjusted to facilitate proper tuning of each string, without interfering with simultaneous tension variation of the several strings required to produce a tremolo effect".

The 3rd paragraph refers to the fully adjustable bridge (described in a later section), which was then construed as an integral part of the vibrato device so that it could be protected by the same patent. Back in 1954, the Fender Synchronized Tremolo was far superior to anything available on the market, but to have it players were then compelled to purchase the new Stratocaster guitar. By all means, it was not meant to be a mere add-on accessory, like the Bigsby unit, but a key structural feature of a radically innovative instrument.

Thanks to the patent drawings and abundant wording (3 pages), the 2nd issue of the Synchronized Tremolo is well documented. Besides, one just has to examine a pre-1972 Stratocaster to grasp the original design. Unfortunately, no picture nor any drawing of the first vibrato devised by Leo Fender, ever surfaced to grace the encyclopaedia of FENDER memorabilia (and this book !).

The "Comfort Contour Body"

Along with the Tremolo unit, the "Comfort Contour Body" was the other striking feature of the Stratocaster in 1954. Even though the concept was quite radical for its time, its origins are fairly straightforward and,

The other Fender "Firsts"

Leo Fender's prime objective was to design a vibrato, which would return to pitch and stay in tune. It was therefore logical for him to also spare some thoughts on straight intonation problems. Back in 1953, Fender solid bodies were equipped with fairly rudimentary (and cheap) bridges, featuring only one saddle to compensate for two strings at a time. Now, as Freddie Tavares puts it: **"Some musicians have musical ears that you just can't believe and others don't. So, it was inevitable that somebody would complain about the fact that we used one bridge for two strings, because a string cannot be in tune with itself on a guitar without a special allowance beyond the string length"** (26). Bill Carson is keen to recall: **"Another thing about the Telecaster that I didn't like was the fact that there were compromises over three bridges and you couldn't intonate it"** (27). The Fender sales force probably mentioned that a rather

primitive intonation capacity was not on par with the lofty goals pursued by the Company to help working musicians. At some stage, Don Randall might have asked Leo to correct this "minus selling proposition", just like he had asked him in 1950 to put a truss rod in the neck of the Esquire/Broadcaster!

Anyway, Leo Fender devised a new bridge featuring 6 individual saddles so that each string's intonation could be dealt with separately. In accordance with previous Fender bridges, saddles were adjustable in height and length, but they were given a new shape in order to increase stability with the vibrato action. Height adjustment was performed with 2 small Allen screws, whilst the adequate string length was achieved by a Philips screw, inserted in the rear flange of the bridge base plate. This novel bridge design was incorporated in the "Synchronized Tremolo" patent filed in August 1954, hence the words "FENDER" and "PAT.PEND." stamped on each saddle of the production models.

Was the Stratocaster the first commercially produced guitar fitted with such a fully adjustable bridge ? Probably yes, if height and length adjustment for each string is taken into account since the Stratocaster bridge was then the only unit enabling the player to custom adjust the strings radius over the fretboard. For the sake of the record, it should be noted that on the earliest version of the bridge, the intonation screws came from the pickup side and not from the rear end of the bridge. The breadboard model was first fitted with this "reverse" adjustment, until Bill Carson complained to Leo Fender that it was not practical in a job situation. The adjusting screws were therefore displaced, before the new guitar made it to the production line.

On the contrary, the reason why the Stratocaster was equipped with 3 pickups seems to have little to do with sheer "musical" requirements. Sound-wise, the wants and needs of mid-1950's players were still rather conservative and the 3-pickup assembly is the result of a combination of elements.

The simplest explanation offered by Leo Fender himself is that he used 3 pickups, because he had in stock 3-position selector switches ! On the other hand, it can be reckoned that Mr Fender may have wanted to foster the unique and superior image of his new guitar, just like a car manufacturer adds chrome and other flashy attributes to its top models. Fredie Tavares remembers : **"Leo said it's quite a thing to have 2 pickups now, so let's have 3 !"** (28). Historically speaking though, this was not really a "first" since in 1949 GIBSON had already introduced the ES-5 hollow body electric with 3 pickups. Such an appointment probably did not go unnoticed by the Fender sales force and Don Randall might have suggested that 3 pickups could be a "plus" in terms of marketing tactics. At that time, GIBSON was catching onto the solid body concept, with its Les Paul model and Electric Bass, and FENDER was certainly keen to retain its leadership in this field.

The 3-position selector switch available in 1953 only allowed the choice of one pickup at a time and no one anticipated the 2-pickup combinations so much favoured by today's players. Freddie Tavares concedes : **"We were not omnipotent enough in our minds to realize that the switch could be more versatile !"** (29), while Leo Fender once said in an interview : **"There weren't too many convenient styles of switches back then. It wasn't a matter of what we would like so much as it was a matter of what we could get to work with !"** (30).

Although it remained fairly straightforward, the wiring circuit of the new guitar reflected the use of 3 pickups in displaying 3 distinct controls next to the selector switch, i.e. a master volume control and two tone controls for the neck and the middle pickups only. It was considered that the lead pickup near the bridge did not require any kind of tone correction if it was to deliver a very bright sound. In those days, amplifiers were rather deficient at the top end and the Stratocaster lead pickup was thus meant to give "clear ringing highs". This is why it was actually placed in a slanted position, so that it could produce a better tone. Freddie Tavares explains : **"The rear pickup is slanted for a very important reason. That was because when you pluck the instrument way back near the bridge, everything is more brilliant, but you lose the depth. So, the reason for the slant was to get a little more vitality or "virility" into the bass strings and still maintain all the brilliance that we wanted"** (31).

The specifications of the pickups were determined through trial and error and Leo Fender made several units for Bill Carson to try out at gigs and in studio sessions. Again, Freddie Tavares remembers : **"When it came to choosing the size of wire and how many turns, that was totally empirical... wind more, wind less and then try it ! We did a lot of empirical experimenting, you know, and of course the final arbiter with everything was Leo"** (32). Mr Fender thus tested a wide variety of pickup configurations, with different coils and polepieces, until he found one which he liked better. Such experiments explain why the Stratocaster pickups were initially wound with a fractionally thinner wire than the Telecaster. Besides, unlike the earlier Telecaster pickups, they were built with staggered polepieces of different heights, so as to accomodate the varying output of each string gauge. In other words, the stronger the output, the shorter the Alnico polepiece in order to optimize the overall balance of the pickup. Bearing in mind the usual (heavy) string gauges of the time, Leo Fender initially ranked the size of the polepieces as follows (shortest to tallest) : B – E (treble) – G – E (bass) – A and D strings. The staggered polepieces were not meant, by and large, to be a "unique selling proposition" in 1954, as a number of guitars were already sporting adjustable polepieces. Actually, it should rather be viewed as a design intended to mitigate some of the shortcomings of the earlier Telecaster pickups, such as a particularly loud B string. Shielding, howewer, was not deemed then as a critical issue and it was not attempted to use metal pickup covers.

The surface-mounted jack receptacle was conceived both as a convenient and a pretty appointment. The basic idea was to put the plug in a safer place, so that a plugged-in guitar could conveniently stand up against a wall or a chair during a short break. A top-mounted plug was also considered to be more conspicuous and players would no longer have to grope for it on the edge of the body. Like the other controls on the Stratocaster, it was meant to be within reach of the player's hands, as acknowledged by Leo Fender : **"Another very important consideration was the position of the controls. On the Stratocaster we positioned them a lot nearer the guitarist's playing hand and that seemed very popular"** (33).

Last but not least, beyond all technical innovations, the Stratocaster also introduced another very significant "first" : the all-time classic Fender headstock ! Leo Fender has recalled on many occasions how he came up with the idea of an asymetric peghead, featuring 6 in-line tuners on one side. Technically speaking, he wanted to put the strings in a straight line to the tuning machines and not fan them out like on a regular guitar. Aesthetically speaking, he made it clear that he drew inspiration from Croatian instruments of Eastern Europe origine. The Telecaster headstock was a primitive expression of this concept, with just enough wood to affix the tuners and stick a brand label. Freddie Tavares remembers : **"The Telecaster had a minimum head. Just enough to hold the thing, with a little curve up there. Just enough to keep it from looking, too dog-gone square ! Now, it was time to make the head a little nicer"** (34).

Both Leo and Freddie went on to design the Stratocaster headstock, characterized by its sharper lower extension and rounder upper bout. This newer style peghead soon became a world famous hallmark for the Company, as it was later adopted, albeit with slight variances, on nearly all the Fender guitars and basses, except the Telecaster. An interesting argument about this popular design is that it looks like a smoothed-out version of the peghead used by P.A. Bigsby on his own guitars in the late 1940's. Paul Bigsby, a Southern California resident living in Downey, came to fame after inventing the vibrato tailpiece which bears his name. On several occasions, [renowned country picker and singer] Merle Travis clearly expressed the view that "he designed the Fender guitar", because in his eyes the Broadcaster was obviously influenced by the guitar Paul Bigsby had custom-built for him upon his specifications. Understandably, Leo Fender always disagreed with such a blunt statement and an enduring controversy broke out between the two gentlemen for decades. The author will not attempt to state the case and decide who is right in this matter, but the fact is that the Stratocaster peghead bears a close resemblance to the design used by Paul Bigsby as early as 1947. Having said that, it became popular world wide on Fender guitars...

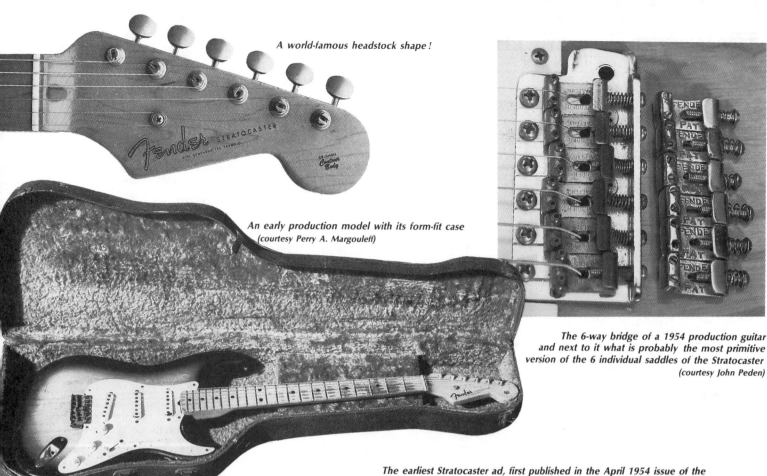

A world-famous headstock shape!

An early production model with its form-fit case
(courtesy Perry A. Margouleff)

The 6-way bridge of a 1954 production guitar
and next to it what is probably the most primitive
version of the 6 individual saddles of the Stratocaster
(courtesy John Peden)

The earliest Stratocaster ad, first published in the April 1954 issue of the
International Musician magazine.

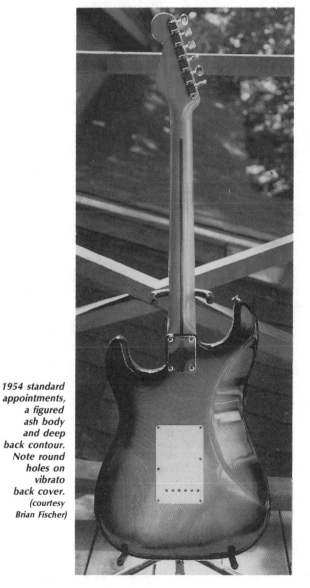

1954 standard
appointments,
a figured
ash body
and deep
back contour.
Note round
holes on
vibrato
back cover.
(courtesy
Brian Fischer)

FROM PROTOTYPE TO PRODUCTION

According to Freddie Tavares and Bill Carson – and contrary to Leo Fender's recollections on the subject – the Stratocaster gradually took shape in the course of 1953. The overall development of the new guitar, from the drawing board up to the early production models required less than a year and a big portion of that time was devoted to fixing the first tremolo unit. No-one seems able, however, to remembrer how many prototypes were built during that period. Owing to the typical Fender assembly mode, it would appear that no more than two "breadboard" models were actually used before the specifications were finalized.

Bill Carson recalls that he started to fieldtest the prototype around the Summer of 1953 in clubs and recording sessions. At the time, it was nicknamed the "Carson guitar", as no official designation had yet been assigned to the new instrument. This early prototype had no finish on the body and it was sporting a black fibreboard pickguard to hold the pickups and the metal knobs "à la" Telecaster. Bill Carson specifies: **"As far as I remember, the breadboard model had a fiberboard pickguard. It was out of the same material as the pickup coil forms were made. Then, after that, there was an anodized aluminum pickguard, but it turned your hands black, so we went to a single ply white pickguard"** (35). Unfortunately, no picture of this "breadboard model" is apparently available today and to make things rough, nobody has seen a genuine prototype of the Stratocaster guitar since the 1950's. Back then, Leo Fender may have documented in writing some of the evolutionary stages of his new guitar, but there is today no Holy Relics to show to the children's children of the pioneers of rock weaponry! Anyway, by the end of 1953, what may temporarily have been the "Carson guitar" definitely became the new Fender electric Spanish guitar. It was then time to care for the appearance of the model.

Unlike the Company's previous electrics, the standard finish retained for the guitar was not the light coloured "Blonde", but a deep sunburst shading. Two major reasons may have accounted for the choice of what was then an unusual finish at FENDER. First, the sales forces was no doubt keen to differentiate the Stratocaster from the Telecaster by giving it an exclusive finish. Fair enough, but why then sunburst, otherwise quite common on several guitars at the time ? From a marketing point of view, a sunburst shading was perhaps viewed as a concession towards a more traditional approach, likely to appeal to new categories of players. The second reason is rooted in manufacturing constraints. Fender instruments were then made out of 2 or 3 pieces of ash and one-piece bodies were pretty much the exception, as the factory could not obtain wide enough planks of wood. Grain was showing through the semi transparent Blonde finish and some bookmatching was necessary to disguise the seal between the pieces. Bodies were also carefully sprayed on the edges, so that wood lamination would not appear too conspicuous. Bearing in mind those parameters, a dark sunburst finish was certainly more convenient and it allowed slight inconsistencies between production guitars.

Leo Fender was keen on an aluminium pickguard because he liked the material and he felt it was both pretty and purposeful. Despite the plating problem mentioned by Bill Carson (hands turning black !), a handful of early models were nevertheless released with gold anodized pickguards, but a single ply white pickguard was retained as the basic trim on production guitars. This brought about a change in the (metal) knobs and matching white knobs were selected in a supplier's catalogue. In 1954, Leo Fender also produced a very few Stratocasters featuring a clear Lucite pickguard with gold paint underneath.

The new guitar was ready to make its official debut, but it still needed a designation. Latest investigations have it that the "Stratocaster" name was not coined by Leo Fender, but by Donald Randall then president of FENDER SALES Inc. It was meant to blend a modern space-age "stratospheric" appeal, quite trendy in the 1950's, with the catchy "caster" suffix. Now, the next big question deals with the exact date of introduction of the Stratocaster. According to the Leo Fender : **"We had the new action developed beginning in 1953 and we started supplying Strats about the Summer of '53"** (36). In another interview, he went on to say : **"We started supplying Stratocasters around the end of 1953"** (37). Freddie Tavares does not share the same recollection and declares : **"We saw the first Stratocasters in early 1954. I don't think we sold any Stratocasters until after the end of the year [1953]"** (38). Mr Fender is probably off by a year or so, because who has ever seen a genuine 1953 Stratocaster ? He was perhaps referring to some pre-production guitars, intended for additional fieldtesting around the end of 1953.

Actual production began during the 1st quarter of 1954 and the very first advertisement about the Stratocaster only appeared in the April issue of the "INTERNATIONAL MUSICIAN" magazine. A reproduction of the ad was immediately sent to FENDER dealers with a note of information, specifying that "shipments are expected to begin May 15".

In its early ads, FENDER was announcing the new Stratocaster with these words :

"Another first for FENDER ! First again in the field of amplified music... the thrilling new "Stratocaster" by FENDER ! Years ahead in design... unequaled in performance ! You've a new thrill in store for you when you play this revolutionary new instrument".

The guitar was also brought to the attention of the music industry in an article published in the May issue of the "MUSIC TRADES" magazine, which indicated :

"The most revolutionary feature of this new instrument is its 'comfort contoured' body design, which actually seems to make the guitar a part of the player and affords more playing comfort than ever before".

The wording of the first catalogue entry of the Stratocaster was in the same vein, as in the 1950's the description of an instrument was rather succinct by modern standards, and least of all technical. Like other guitar manufacturers, FENDER was then more inclined to simply stress the innovative features of its products and outline the fact that they were meant to suit the needs of discerning professional players ! In 1954, this attitude prompted a few "gems" in catalogue literature such as :

"The tone of the Stratocaster guitar is as new and different as tomorrow and is that big professional tone so long sought after by critical players"
"The Stratocaster is truly an artist's guitar and combines all the fine features of the original Fender solid body guitars plus the many new developments which make it the most advanced instrument on the market".

Now, the major difference with other similar assertions, found in a lot of catalogue descriptions, is that time has shown all these statements to be perfectly true !! It is safe to say that the Fender sale people who wrote them in 1954 certainly did not anticipate the prodigious impact of the Stratocaster over the next 4 decades.

At the time of its introduction, the Stratocaster with "Synchronized Tremolo" listed for $249.50 (without case). By comparison, the GIBSON Les Paul Custom and Les Paul Model respectively listed for $325 and $225 (without case) in September 1954, while the sister Telecaster was going for $189.50. The early Stratocasters were sold in a hardshell case, with a simulated brown leather covering and red plush lining, costing an additional $39.95.

Although the new vibrato was one of its strongest marketing assets, the Stratocaster was also introduced without a "Synchronized Tremolo" in 1954. The non-Tremolo Stratocaster was slightly less expensive and listed for $ 229.50 (without case). It was built with the same string-through-body system as the Telecaster, but it retained the 6-way bridge for proper intonation. Throughout the years, the "non-trem" variant was obviously produced in lesser quantities than the regular guitar with vibrato, but it was continuously listed by FENDER until 1984. This being said, only a handful of Stratocasters without Tremolo were actually produced in 1954.

The Stratocaster has undoubtedly stood the test of time. But, although it allegedly retained the same basic specifications over the years, players and collectors are quick to point out the numerous details which distinguish the many variants of the model since 1954. This modern cult following has helped create and sustain the legend and has also given birth to a searching "Strat-anthology", adequately enhanced by its own icons and semantics.

ANNOUNCING THE NEW
Fender STRATOCASTER
"COMFORT CONTOURED"

ELECTRIC SPANISH GUITAR — WITH OR WITHOUT BUILT IN TREMOLO

Mr. Dealer:

The enclosed advertisement is a reproduction of the inside front cover of the April issue of the International Musician, which reaches approximately 220,000 musicians. This is just another of the many ways in which we, at Fender attempt to build sales for our dealers. You no doubt have already experienced some interest on the part of your local guitar players as a result of this ad.

Now, here are the facts concerning this extremely new and radically different spanish guitar. The Fender Stratocaster represents another "First for the Fender Company" with its "comfort contoured" body and its built-in tremolo. This guitar features a body which is shaped in such a way that, in reality, it becomes a part of the player and is the most comfortable instrument to play ever to be made. It features three highly improved pickups which are, in themselves, adjustable to insure proper tone balance. It has separate tone controls on two of the pickups and a three-position tone changing switch which gives instant response to any one of three pre-determined tone colorings.

The Stratocaster Guitar also featuressa surface mounted plug receptacle, which virtually ends the old hassle due to cord and plug interference. This feature alone, will be welcomed by all electric guitar players. Each string is individually adjustable for action or height from the fret board and for length, which insuress true fretting or pitch. This sectional bridge is a patented feature which no other guitar on the market today can duplicate.

Probably the foremost of the features of this new instrument is the built-in mechanical tremolo. This guitar is the first to appear on the market with its own built-in tremolo and while devices of this nature have been available in the past, as accessories, they have all been very weak in their effectiveness. The Fender tremolo provides easy action and a full tone change, both above and below the basic tuning, plus the fact that the guitar will remain in tune even after long playing with the tremolo, a feature which none of the other tremolo accessories, so far, have been able to duplicate. The tone of this instrument is extremely fine and variable within wide limits. Another feature which every qualified guitar player will recognize is this guitar's ability to sustain a note. Many instruments are very dead in this respect, which causes the player to have to work exceptionally hard to get the type of response he is seeking.

The price of the guitar with tremolo is $249.50. It is available without tremolo at $229.50. The case, which is of hardshell construction, crushed plush lined, with ample padding and covered in a grain hair seal simulated leather covering is available at $39.95.

You will undoubtedly experience a great deal of interest concerning this instrument, so place your orders now. Shipments are expected to begin May 15. When placing your orders for this guitar, do not forget that Fender Amplifiers are the standard by which all others are judged, so be sure to have a wide variety on hand at all times.

Facsimile of the letter sent by Fender Sales Inc. to its dealers. The last paragraph stipulates that "shipments are expected to begin May 15" (courtesy Richard Smith)

Excerpt from the May 1954 issue of the Music Trades magazine.

Fender Sales Features New Stratocaster Guitar

Donald D. Randall, Fender president, claims another "Fender First" in the solid body Spanish electric guitar — the new Fender Stratocaster guitar, with its built-in tremolo and its comfort contoured body, one of the most revolutionary of the amplified string instruments.

It features the same steel reinforced, fast action neck that has become so widely known on Fender guitars. It incorporates three advanced-style pickups with appropriate tone and volume controls and tone changing lever-type switch. Its surface mounted plug receptacle is an entirely new feature in this field and one which all musicians will recognize and welcome as a big advantage. This prevents cord breakage, allows the instrument to be set up in any position and puts the jack in plain view of the player, so he doesn't have to hunt for it.

The most revolutionary features of this new instrument are its "comfort contoured" body design which actually seems to make the guitar a part of the player and affords more playing comfort than ever before. This is a feature which must be seen and tried to be appreciated.

The built-in tremolo is of an advanced design. It has the advantages of giving a full 1½ - 2 tone variation in pitch and is easily operated. The tremolo actuating lever can remain in the player's hand regardless of the picking position or movement of the picking hand and is always ready for instant use.

Mr. Randall believes that this instrument will revolutionize the style of guitar playing. The body is beautifully finished with a sunburst effect, while the neck is of a natural finish rock maple. It comes complete with a tooled leather strap and shoulder pad.

The Stratocaster is available either with or without the tremolo mechanism and it is felt that practically every professional performer will want one of these new instruments. For further information, write Fender Sales, Inc., 308 E. 5th St., Santa Ana, Calif.

1954 SPECIFICATIONS

NECK
- one-piece detachable Hard Rock maple neck
- asymetric peghead with 6 in-line nickel-plated Kluson tuners
- straight string pull to the tuners
- round string retainer for the top E and B strings
- reinforcement metal truss rod, adjustable at the body end of the neck
- 4-bolt mounting onto the body with a tempered steel anchor plate
- 25 1/2" scale length
- fretboard radius = 7"
- standard nut width = 1,625"
- 21 nickel-silver frets
- black dot position markers at the 3rd, 5th, 7th, 9 th, 12th (double), 15th, 17th, 19th and 21st frets.

BODY
- figured light ash body
- deep double cutaway shape
- exclusive "comfort contour" design, with a relief in the back and under the armrest to fit the player's body
- neck-to-body junction near the 16th fret
- dimensions = 18" (length) × 12,750" (width) × 1,750" (depth).

PICKUPS & CONTROLS
- 3 single coil pickups featuring :
  - 6 staggered polepieces for an improved string response
  - 6 cylindrical Alnico 5 magnets (Dia. = .192")
  - ca. 8350 turns of 42AWG heavy formvar wire
  - a nominal DC resistance of ca.6K Ohms
- pickup elevating screws located at either end of pickups
- slanted lead pickup for improved output near the bridge
- master volume control (250K Ohm pot)
- tone controls (250K Ohm pots with .1Mfd capacitor) for the neck and middle pickups
- 3-position pickup selector switch.

HARDWARE
- 2-way adjustable bridge section, with 6 individual string saddles for proper intonation
- built-in "Synchronized Tremolo" with swing-away arm and adjustable tension springs
- single ply white pickguard with 8 mounting screws
- white control knobs with a 0 to 10 graduation
- surface-mounted jack receptacle
- nickel-plated strap holders
- all metal parts with heavy chrome plating unless otherwise specified.

FINISH
- neck : sealed with clear nitro-cellulose lacquer
- body : nitro-cellulose 2-tone dark sunburst shading.

ACCESSORIES
- brown form-fit hard case with red plush lining
- adjustable leather strap and shielded cord.

40 YEARS OF STRATOCASTERS. AN OVERVIEW

The Stratocaster success story can be divided into 6 distinct periods spanning from the 1950's to the 1990's. Such a bias appears justified in the light of some of the fundamental features of the model during each of these 6 periods. But, it does also refer to the 3 major eras thus far in the FENDER history: the Leo Fender years up to 1964, the C.B.S. affiliation from 1965 until early 1985, and the more recent «post-C.B.S.» era under the guidance of Bill Schultz and Dan Smith.

1954 - 1959

The first period, dealing with the early years of the model, could be subtitled either **« ORIGINAL ISSUE WITH A MAPLE NECK »** or **« PRE-CBS WITH A MAPLE NECK »**. For those not yet familiar with the lexicon of elementary Fenderology, the second title refers to the (in) famous CBS takeover is early 1965. Both captions acknowledge the fact that during its first 5 years the Stratocaster was exclusively fitted with the fretted one-piece maple neck (« Maple Neck » for short) pioneered by LEO FENDER.

From its official debut in April 1954 until about June 1959, the basic appointments of the Stratocaster can be summarized as follows :

1 one-piece Maple Neck with 21 frets.
2 « small » headstock.
3 old style Fender logo (a.k.a. « spaghetti logo »).
4 nickel-plated Kluson tuning keys.
5 4-bolt neck mounting.
6 truss rod adjustment at the body end of the neck.
7 2-piece vibrato tailpiece with separate inertia block.
8 nickel-plated steel bridge saddles with a Fender stamp.
9 single ply white pickguard with 8 mounting screws.
10 3 single coil pickups with staggered polepieces.
11 deeply comfort-contoured ash body (alder standard after 1956).
12 nitro- cellulose lacquer finish.

Based on crosschecked information available today, production of the Stratocaster at a factory level probably began in March 1954. Asked about a date, GEORGE FULLERTON remembers that : **« It was no later than March 1954 »** (39). Shipments from the factory, however, did not take place until about two months later, as suggested by the circular then sent by FENDER SALES INC. to its dealers stipulating that **« SHIPMENTS ARE EXPECTED TO BEGIN MAY 15 »**. As it was often the case at FENDER in those days, production started at a rather moderate pace both because of marketing and manufacturing considerations. At the time, the music industry heavily relied on the Summer NAMM convention as its focal point in the year to introduce new products. Although the Stratocaster was first advertised in April 1954, the FENDER sales force was probably keen to test its dealers' reaction (and take orders !) at the forthcoming NAMM show before committing itself to any production schedule. On the other hand, it certainly took some time as well for the factory to tool up and standardize manufacturing operations for the new guitar. Some Stratocasters were made in the first half of 1954, but they were basically intended for promotion, artist endorsement and also FENDER most daring dealers. According to FORREST WHITE, who was hired by Leo Fender in May 1954 as plant manager, full-scale production did not begin until October, when a batch of 100 guitars was first put on a single order by FENDER SALES INC. Yet, in July 1954, 200 unfinished bodies and 150 unfinished necks were already held in stock to meet initial orders.

The earliest Stratocasters released in Spring of 1954 shared a few specific features which were later discontinued in the course of Summer. For instance, FENDER dropped the original control knobs after a few months and opted for slightly taller units with a different skirt. At the same time, the original pearl white bakelite material, initially used for the knobs and the pickup covers, was discarded because it often cracked. It was replaced by a « mattish » and more durable white material, which remained in use until about 1956 before FENDER again changed in favour of white ABS plastic less prone to wearing off on the edges. The earliest pickup covers are characterized by their rounded edges and glossier appearance. The serial number was moved from the vibrato backplate onto the neck plate by the end of June, after the Company certainly realized that backplates were not always kept screwed-on by players wishing to do a quick restringing. It was not until early 1955, however, that the round holes on the backplate were changed for oblong holes. Finally, a couple of early '54 Stratocasters were released with a gold anodized metal pickguard.

The original 'form fit' case was also dropped during Summer 1954 and replaced by the first of the 'tweed case' series. The 'centre pouch' or 'centre pocket' tweed case was kept until early 1955 and then replaced, probably on cost grounds, by the standard shape FENDER case with a pocket in the lower left hand corner. 1955 is also the year when a snap-on bridge cover was first made available on the guitar and when non-tremolo models began to be produced in quantity. According to FORREST WHITE'S personal files, they accounted for about 20 % of the overall production of Stratocasters during that year.

Some Stratocasters from the 1950's may have nicely figured Maple Necks but it is rather coincidental in the factory wood supply and in no way a custom appointment. Actually, LEO FENDER was not keen on such « extras » as indicated by FREDDIE TAVARES : **« Leo always discouraged the beautiful wood in the neck because it's so rare. If we were a custom instruments' maker, fine, we could get enough of it, but not to make plenty of guitars. So, Leo was very much against it, because it is not a good thing to do to have the ordinary run of the mill products to look like superlative instruments now and then for the same price »** (40). This attitude may also explain why bodies were made out of alder instead of ash after late 1956. Ash is a beautiful hardwood, often heavily figured albeit fairly inconsistent, and LEO FENDER probably experienced problems in maintaining a standard supply of the same quality. Alder is less expensive and easier to obtain in quantity and it was no doubt reckoned to be more convenient for production purposes, because it is easier to seal and its lack of figured grain does not require any specific bookmatching. Ash was not totally discarded though and it was retained on the custom-coloured guitars, especially on the Blond(e) Stratocasters because this translucent finish adequately showcased its grain.

When it was introduced in 1954, the Stratocaster was theoretically available in sunburst finish only. However, as recalled by FREDDIE TAVARES : **« Some people in show business, especially country people, asked for solid colours. There was for instance this fellow, HANK PENNY was his name, he had a band in Las Vegas where he played the lounges, not the big shows. A very funny guy... he wanted a purple one ! »** (41). Likewise, ELDON SHAMBLIN (veteran of Bob Wills and his Texas Playboys and Leon Mc Auliffe's band) asked for a gold-painted Stratocaster and BILL CARSON chose to have his production guitar finished in red. Bill remembers : **« It was called Cimarron Red, the reason being that LEON MC AULIFFE, a steel-guitar player who had a working arrangement with Leo Fender for many years, liked that particular finish. The name actually came from the Cimarron Ballroom in Tulsa, Oklahoma. That's a big ballroom that Leon owned and that's where his band was. He picked out the paint, sent it to Leo and called it Cimarron Red. So, we had that particular finish there and I had one Stratocaster painted for me in that colour »** (42).

Custom colours - i.e. non-standard specific finishes - were thus used at factory level as early as 1954 to satisfy the requests of a handful of playing

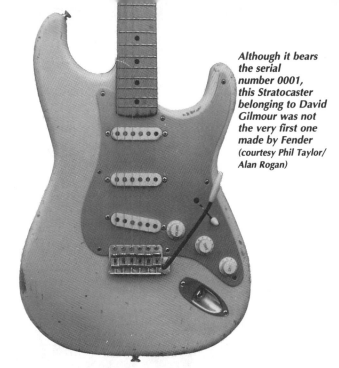

Although it bears the serial number 0001, this Stratocaster belonging to David Gilmour was not the very first one made by Fender (courtesy Phil Taylor/ Alan Rogan)

Howard Reed playing his custom-ordered '55 black Stratocaster during his stint with the Blue Caps. (courtesy James Werner)

A pair of '54 models with original hardcases. The guitar on the left (neck date 7-54) is lying in a form-fit case, while the one on the right (neck date 8-54) rests in a centre-pouch case. (courtesy "Uncle Lou" Gatanas)

A December 1956 ad, featuring Buddy Merrill with his Stratocaster

A promotional shot of Gene Vincent and his band, the Blue Caps, with Blonde Stratocasters.

*One of the ads from the very successful late 50's campaign
(Guess the type of the aircraft!)*

You won't part with yours either

Where musicians go, you'll find Fender!

Fender
SALES INC.

INTERNATIONAL MUSICIAN

*A mint
1959
model*

*Buddy Holly, undoubtedly the first Strat'
hero on top of a very long list*

*1957 non-trem
Stratocaster in Blonde*

1961 guitar with rosewood "slab" board

artists. By 1956, a « custom colour » option first appeared in print at the bottom page of the Fender catalogue, stipulating that « STRATOCASTER GUITARS ARE AVAILABLE IN DU-PONT DUCCO COLORS OF THE PLAYER'S CHOICE AT AN ADDITIONAL 5 % COST ». In fact, this option was not exercised by many players as most of them were then rather conservative in their approach to guitar finishes.

In February 1957, FENDER officially announced a 'deluxe' version of the Stratocaster, finished inBlond(e) with 14 Carat gold-plated parts, at a $ 330 listprice plus case. Although it was not advertised previously, Blond(e) Stratocasters were actually produced since the introduction of the model in 1954 as the well- known creamy off-white finish was the standard trim on other Fender electrics. In the 1958-59 catalogue the colour option was rephrased to mention that « THE STRATOCASTER IS AVAILABLE IN CUSTOM COLORS OR BLOND FINISH AT AN ADDITIONAL 5 % COST ». In other words, optional colours were no longer of the player's choice as before because FENDER was beginning to put together its own palette of « standardized custom » finishes. GEORGE FULLERTON vividly recalls : **« One day, I went down to a local paint store and I started to explain to the man what I had in mind. I had him mix some paint there on the spot and finally we came up with a red colour. That was what got the colour thing started and that particular red became Fiesta Red. In England, that was the only colour they bought for a long time. They weren't ordering anything else, but that Fiesta Red ! »** (43). Asked about a date, George goes on to specify : **« I would say probably late 1957/early 1958. The custom colours came out about the time the Jazzmaster just came out. The reason I know that is because I had the colour red put over one of the early manufactured Jazzmasters. I still have the instrument as a matter of fact »** (44).

The Fiesta Red finish was then prominently displayed on the front cover of the 1958-59 catalogue, but sprayed on a Stratocaster as the Jazzmaster did not make it on the cover (although it was featured inside the catalogue as the new top model). Thirty years ago, it was no doubt unusual - to say the least - to paint a professional guitar in red, but as GEORGE FULLERTON is keen to add: **«No-one was making colored instruments back then, so it was an opportunity for us to do something different and it turned out pretty nice»** (45). Besides, according to FREDDIE TAVARES: **«Public demand made Leo consider it»** (46). At any rate, the advent of solid custom colors was certainly fostered in the late 1950's by the emergence of rock and roll as well as a thriving car culture in the U.S.A. In fact, the finishes offered by FENDER were more than often automotive paints and a Stratocaster in Fiesta Red was a good match for a '58 Corvette finished in Cardinal Red. Overall, though, custom finishes did not become real popular until the early 1960's and, in terms of numbers, only a few Stratocasters were sprayed with solid colors in the late 1950's (hence their usually 'stratospheric' price today on the vintage market!). Judging from original Stratocasters available today, Fiesta Red and Shoreline Gold Metallic were certainly the most popular custom colors in the late 1950's.

Meanwhile, the regular 2-tone sunburst shading was altered to include some red blended between black and yellow. This change probably occurred at the request of the FENDER sales force, which may have spotted the need for a brighter finish. The 2-tone sunburst shading was abandoned by FENDER in early 1958, but a fair number of late 50's and very early 60's Strats look today as if they were painted with a 2-tone sunburst. So what ?

In fact, the « 2-tone » Strats of the late 50's were actually finished in a 3-tone sunburst at the factory, but due to some chemical interaction the red stain did not last after the guitar was exposed to daylight for some time. GIBSON was confronted by the same problem in those days, noticeably on its 1958 and 1959 Les Paul Standard, and the Kalamazoo company had to change its red colour pigment to achieve a lasting 3-tone sunburst shading, such as the one found on most 1960 Standards. Without immediately noticing it, FENDER probably suffered a change in its supplies of colour pigments and it affected the stability of the red in the 3-tone sunburst finish. BILL CARSON remembers : **« We had to search and so we sprayed many blocks of alder and put them on the top of the building to see which ones would fade and which ones wouldn't ! the red just simply got gobbled up in this chemical interaction »** (47).

The Stratocaster basically underwent few other modifications until mid-1959, except that the neck profile changed in accordance with players' requirements. The round clubby neck of the earliest guitars was

replaced by a « V » profile («boat neck ») after 1955, which in turn was superseded by a much slimmer profile in mid-1958. Finally, it should also be mentioned that a very few Stratocasters were again fitted with an anodized metal pickguard in 1958, as FENDER was using then the same material to ornate other models such as the Jazzmaster, Musicmaster, Duo-Sonic and Precision Bass.

During the 1954-1959 period, the Stratocaster was at first mainly considered as a country and western instrument, both because of its natural 'twangy' sound and also because of the regular FENDER clientele at the time. Nevertheless, for the nation-wide promotion of the Stratocaster, FENDER SALES INC. initially relied on BUDDY MERRILL, then featured guitarist with the Lawrence Welk Dance Band, in an effort to give a broader and less specific exposure to the model. Beginning in 1957, FENDER opted for a less personalized type of ads and the guitar was prominently featured in a highly humoristic campaign under the headline « You won't part with yours either ». It is fair to say that true recognition of the Stratocaster uniqueness was triggered by rock and roll and some of its aspiring talents in the mid-to-late 1950's. In this respect BUDDY HOLLY, whose renown helped to set the guitar on its fabulous course, has to be acknowledged as the first « Strat hero ».

1959 - 1965

The obvious title for the 1959-1965 period is **« PRE-CBS WITH A ROSEWOOD FRETBOARD »**, because 1959 is the year when the original one-piece Maple Neck was (temporarily) suspended on the Stratocaster and replaced by a more conventional 2-piece neck with a separate rosewood cap.
Although such a significant change affected the Stratocaster in 1959, its seeds actually go back to the previous year when the Jazzmaster guitar was officially introduced at the July 1958 NAMM convention in Chicago. The Jazzmaster was indeed the first ever Fender production instrument fitted with a glued-on rosewood fretboard in lieu of the usual one-piece Maple Neck. Two major reasons accounted for such a change, which in any case was triggered by DON RANDALL and FENDER SALES INC. as recalled by GEORGE FULLERTON : **« I think it was a request from the sales office, probably from Don Randall »** (48) or by FREDDIE TAVARES : **« As I remember, our distributors which were a different entity [FENDER SALES INC.] would come up from time to time with suggestions because they had their ideas and thoughts on marketing. They wanted a rosewood fingerboard. They said : everybody else has one, why can't we have one ? »** (49). The Jazzmaster was then meant to become the new top model at FENDER and the sales force may have decided that it would be appropriate to give it a more conventional fretboard to conquer a new breed of customers. Another reason is also put forward by BILL CARSON : **« Another thing that influenced the decision to opt for rosewood was that, in those days, we didn't have the polyesters for material on the neck and the lacquer wore through very rapidly on a maple neck. Then it became discoloured and it also started to wear into the wood »** (50).

By 1959 the decision had been made at FENDER to switch the whole range of electrics to a rosewood fretboard. As per standard practice then in the industry, the modification was carried out to become effective by the Summer of 1959. Therefore, from July 1959 until November 1965, the basic appointments of the Stratocaster can be summarized as follows : (NB : * shows a change compared to previous period).

1 * two-piece neck with a 21-fret rosewood board glued over maple.
2 « small » headstock.
3 * old style Fender logo (discontinued after Fall 1964), then newer « transition »logo (first introduced in July 1964).
4 nickel-plated Kluson tuning keys.
5 4-bolt neck mounting.
6 truss rod adjustment at the body end of the neck.
7 2-piece vibrato tailpiece with separate inertia block.
8 nickel-plated steel bridge saddles with a Fender stamp.
9 * triple ply laminated white pickguard with 11 mounting screws.
10 3 single coil pickups with staggered polepieces.
11 * deeply comfort-contoured body with a gradually shorter back relief.
12 nitro-cellulose lacquer finish.

During the first few years following the withdrawal of the one-piece Maple Neck, FENDER successively tried different rosewood caps. The earliest version, which was actually devised in 1958 for the Jazzmaster, is milled flat on the neck, hence its current nickname of « slab board » because of its greater amount of wood. It remained in use until July 1962 and then FENDER opted for a thinner rosewood fretboard, pre-contoured or curved underneath to adapt itself on a convex neck base. This second version lasted for about a year and it still showed a reasonable amount of rosewood despite the change in the neck construction. Finally, it was resolved to streamline the rosewood cap and by mid-1963 the fretboard began to look almost like a veneer over the neck base. This final version remained the standard fretboard trim on the regular Stratocaster (and the other Fender guitars) until 1983.

Such modifications were carried out at the factory in order to strike the best compromise between rosewood and maple, so that both woods would not over-react against each other after being glued. Rosewood has a heavier density and this is why its thickness was ultimately reduced. Besides, a thicker rosewood cap made it more difficult to adjust the built-in truss rod, should the neck begin to warp. It is interesting to note that the first catalogue pictures of the rosewood board Strats show a walnut drop above the nut, like the standard Maple Neck models. This would indicate that on the earliest prototypes with a rosewood cap, the truss rod was installed from the rear of the neck. Of course, production models were fitted with a truss rod installed from the front - i.e. before the rosewood cap is glued - hence the absence of walnut strip (or « skunk stripe ») on the back of the neck.

The change in neck construction somewhat altered the overall sound of the Stratocaster, which then lost some of its crystal clear and ultra brilliant sound trademark. The early 1960's Strats are known indeed for their mellower sound, compared to their 1950's counterparts. It should be mentioned, however, that slight variations in the pickups produced after 1960 tend to magnify the sonic nuances between 1950's and 1960's models. For instance, the hand-guided winding machines were gradually replaced by automatic winders at the factory and it soon affected the number of turns in the coils compared to 1950's units. This is probably why FENDER first referred to « the improved pickups of the Stratocaster » in its 1961-1962 catalogue.

Cosmetically speaking, the advent of the rosewood fretboard coincided with a change in the pickguard. The very first rosewood board Strats released in July/August 1959 still sported the original white single ply unit, certainly to get rid of existing inventories. This was promptly changed in favour of a 3-ply pickguard made out of a new plastic material which gave a distinct 'greenish' tint to the white top layer. This peculiar appointment of the 1959-1964 pickguards is often attributed to ageing, but it actually originated in the plastic material used by FENDER. As a matter of fact, these 3-ply pickguards do not look real white, even on the brand new Stratocasters featured in the early 1960's catalogues. In 1965, the greenish nitrate material was discontinued on safety grounds, because it was highly inflammable and therefore dangerous to store in quantity. In addition to the regular 3-ply white pickguards, some Stratocasters were also fitted throughout the 1960's with a tortoise shell top plate, usually found on guitars finished in sunburst, black or white.

By a twist of fate, the suspension of the Maple Neck also marked the end of the « tweed » cases for the Stratocaster. FENDER kept the same oblong shape, but changed for a brown « Tolex » covering, based on vinyl fabric and made by the General Tire & Rubber Company. By 1963, the brown covering was replaced by a white Tolex covering (with green leather trim) and in 1965 black became the standard outfit for the Stratocaster case.

After 1960, FENDER finally managed to obtain a lasting 3-tone sunburst shading, which showed a much clearer separation between the 3 colours than the original 1958 finish. The first « custom colour chart » was released around 1961 by FENDER, featuring compressed chips of the 14 optional finishes (besides Blond) available from FENDER at a 5 % additional cost. Solid-coloured instruments were produced in larger quantities during the early 1960's, but due to public request, the partition between the various custom finishes was uneven. Some colours did not prove that popular back then and thus were not applied to a lot of guitars. This is probably why FENDER regularly modified its palette of custom finishes to maintain an attractive selection. In spite of the « marketing

plus » brought about by the custom colours, it should be noted that DON RANDALL and FENDER SALES INC. always put the standard sunburst Stratocaster in the forefront in the catalogues, as it was felt to be the most appealing version to the average buyer ! Alder remained the staple wood for the body, with the notable exception of the Blond models as well as occasional solid-coloured instruments. Towards the mid-1960's, a number of Stratocasters were produced with a Mahogany body, probably on an experimental basis, and as such they are quite rare today. After 1960, the body contours began to show marginal reductions both in the back and under the armrest. Since the shaping of the contours was then a man-operated process, it can be assumed that an increased production schedule gradually took its toll among employees in charge of the job. No big deal, but a '57 Strat usually has markedly deeper contours than, say, a '63 model.

Otherwise, the original Fender « spaghetti » logo was dropped from the headstock decal in the course of 1964 and replaced by what is known among collectors as the gold « transition » logo. The new logo first appeared on the Jazz Bass in 1960, but it was not applied to the Stratocaster until 1964. This change probably occurred in an effort to modernize and standardize the corporate image of FENDER, which was no longer a small business but a major corporation in the music industry.

During the early 1960's, the Stratocaster was gradually overshadowed by both the Jazzmaster and then the Jaguar (introduced in 1961). The two guitars with the off-set body design and the 'floating tremolo' unit were prominently featured as the new top electrics and the Stratocaster was soon relegated in third spot in marketing brochures and catalogues. Besides the need to promote in priority its latest top models - which were then substantially more expensive and thus more profitable than the Stratocaster - FENDER also acknowledged the fact that musical trends were heading in new directions. For various well known reasons, rock and roll could not sustain its initial popularity in the U.S.A., where it was then superseded by surf music, folk music and other softer genres like 'italo-rock' ! Be it because of its shape, its sound or its date of creation, the Strat was not deemed to be the right outfit for what were then the commercial forms of music. Of course, it was not totally put on the way-side and a few artists such as DICK DALE, the BEACH BOYS or CURTIS MAYFIELD and the IMPRESSIONS made good use of its sound. Likewise, a young man by the name of BOB DYLAN also resorted to a Stratocaster in 1965 when he felt the need to add some rock shades to his folk music.

In Europe, the SHADOWS, Cliff Richard's backing group, who had released their first instrumental hit 'Apache' in July 1960, were about to pave the way for an intense Strat culture. In the early 1960's Fender instruments were hard to come by in many European countries for lack of proper distributing agreements and it is safe to say that the red Strats of HANK MARVIN and BRUCE WELCH certainly broke new ground for the California-based Company. Thanks to the SHADOWS, England started to order tons of Fiesta Red Stratocasters. Of course, the Fender-mania later gathered more momentum through a host of other British groups, but as far as Europe is concerned the « Shads » really started it all for the Stratocaster.

Back in the mid-1960's though, Europe was not a big enough market to make up for the lagging sales of the Stratocaster in the U.S.A. In August 1965 its listprice was even lowered by a few dollars and, at some stage, FENDER allegedly envisaged dropping the model from its catalogue as it could not match the sales of newcomers like the Mustang. The Stratocaster was NOT discontinued and by a twist of fate this could well be the result of a more important event which took place in late 1964 : the CBS take over.

1965 - 1971

The acquisition of FENDER INSTRUMENTS and FENDER SALES by COLUMBIA BROADCASTING SYSTEMS Inc. (CBS for short) was legally completed to become effective on January 5, 1965 but the deal actually took shape in the course of 1964. The motivations which prompted LEO FENDER - sole owner of FENDER INSTRUMENTS and then 50 % owner of FENDER SALES - and DON RANDALL - then 50 % owner of FENDER SALES - to sell their business are fairly straightforward.

The tremendous success of the Fender products as a whole had been such over the past decade that both Leo and Don had somewhat reached

Skate-rolling Stratocaster, the mid-60's version of "you won't part with yours either"

A rare 1965 model with bound fingerboard (courtesy Perry A. Margouleff)

Dick Dale, the lefty surfer of the Deltones, with his favourite axe (courtesy Fender Musical Instruments)

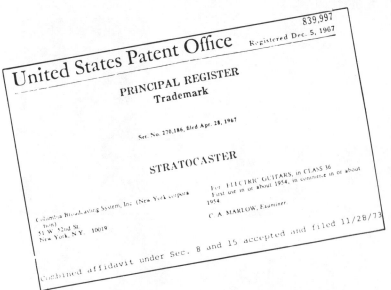

an impasse, whereby more cash was no doubt needed to fuel further expansion. On the other hand, LEO FENDER's health was worsening and he was getting increasingly tired because of a strep infection he had caught during a vacation in the mid-1950's. At some point in time, he decided to quit as he could not work as hard as he wished to and as required by the continuous development of his business. Therefore, Leo asked his accountant, named Wade Tappert, to look for a prospective buyer. The offer which ensued appeared too low in the eyes of DON RANDALL who was allowed by Leo to investigate the market. Don met with representatives from [well-known Wall Street firm] Merrill Lynch, who introduced him to CBS. At that time CBS was willing to divest from its core activities (2 decades later it became the opposite !) and looking for a sound investment to save on its tax bill. Negotiations began in the latter part of Summer 1964 and eventually the FENDER operation was sold for $ 13m.

In the eyes of guitar buffs, the CBS take-over is often considered as THE major turning point in the history of FENDER. Over the years, it has engendered a wealth of stories about a decline in quality, which persisted during the two decades of CBS ownership. It also gave birth to the « PRE-CBS » label which came out to designate the instruments produced before Leo Fender sold out. Now, the main issue under fire is the exact border between pre-CBS and CBS guitars ? Several options can actually fit the bill. The first one simply takes into account the date of completion of the deal - i.e. January 5,1965 - and in this case 1964 is the last of the pre-CBS years. However, changes at production level did not take place on January 6th. Most of the 1965 instruments were manufactured with parts already in stock or built as per the existing production methods. Another deadline often cited is based on the fact that in the course of 1965 neckplates began to be stamped with a backward "F" for Fender. On the whole, this assertion gives a clearer indication, as the big "F" stamped on the neckplate is an adequate symbol of the CBS invasion. In the case of the Stratocaster, however, the true stigma of the CBS take-over is certainly the advent of the enlarged headstock, which first appeared in December 1965. Although this date cannot be used as the border to earmark all of the "CBS" instruments, it is considered by the author as the most appropriate for the Stratocaster. The third period in the Stratocaster story could be dubbed **« CBS EARLY YEARS »** and from December 1965 until about Summer 1971, the basic appointments of the guitar can be summarized as follows :
(NB : * shows a change compared to previous period).

1 * two-piece neck with 21-fret rosewood board glued over maple. Maple board optional after mid-1967, then one-piece Maple Neck optional after mid-1970.
2 * « large » headstock.
3 * gold « transition » logo (discontinued after mid-1968), then newer black logo (first introduced ca.June 1968).
4 * nickel-plated Kluson tuning keys (discontinued in 1967), then Fender chrome-plated tuning keys with « F » stamped on back cover.
5   4-bolt neck mounting.
6   truss rod adjustment at the body end of the neck.
7   2-piece vibrato tailpiece with separate inertia block.
8   nickel-plated steel bridge saddles with a Fender stamp.
9   triple ply white pickguard with 11 mounting screws.
10 3 single coil pickups with staggered polepieces.
11 * medium comfort-contoured body, with a shorter back relief.
12 * nitro cellulose lacquer finish (discontinued ca.1968), then polyester finish.

By the mid-1960's other electrics were surpassing the Stratocaster in terms of numbers and the enlarged peghead was probably a cosmetic attempt to update the looks of the guitar in order to boost its sales. The thin rosewood fretboard remained a basic appointment of the model but by mid-1965 « bound necks » first became available on the Strat after the CBS take-over. The same treatment was inflicted to other electrics such as the Jaguar or the Jazzmaster, albeit with pearloid block inlays instead of dot position markers. The 1966-67 condensed catalogue states that « THE BOUND NECK [of the Stratocaster] HAS THE FAMOUS FENDER TRUSS ROD », whilst the full- colour edition refers to « THE ADVANCED NECK DESIGN WITH BINDING » and shows the pictures of bound-neck Stratocasters in sunburst and Fiesta Red. Although it was depicted as a standard appointment in the above catalogues, neck binding is fairly rare on Stratocasters made between 1965 and 1967. By 1968, the mention was withdrawn from the catalogues.

A more sensible option first appeared in the May 1967 pricelist, whereby a maple fretboard became available at an additional 5 % cost. Actually, a few maple-capped necks were produced before 1967 (and even before CBS took over), but it was truly a custom option which was never heavily publicized. Stratocasters with a maple fretboard were not manufactured in very large quantities between 1967 and 1970, but nevertheless they were used then by prominent Strat players such as JIMI HENDRIX and DAVID GILMOUR. Oldies turning into goldies, the original one-piece Maple Neck was finally re-introduced by popular demand on the threshold of the 1970's. In April 1970, the Stratocaster could be ordered either with a rosewood fretboard for $ 367 or with a Maple Neck for $ 385. Incidentally, left-handed models were also first shown with a different price tag in the April 1970 pricesheet.

Despite the return of the Maple Neck, the years from 1965 to 1970 are to a large extent a transition period during which the Stratocaster surreptitiously drifted away from its pre-CBS configuration, while retaining the same basic specifications. The neck was modified to feature a larger peghead, different position markers (pearloid dots), new Fender tuning gears... the body lost part of its deeply contoured design as well as its nitro-cellulose lacquer finish... the pickup assembly was altered and the coils no longer dipped in wax... the 'greenish' triple ply pickguard was dropped and replaced by a truly white plastic item... shell guards disappeared... optional gold-plated parts were discontinued... All of the above may have been considered then as minor details, but their accumulation progressively gave way to the « PRE-CBS » label, otherwise enforced by an allegedly inferior quality of the products.

By all means, CBS never intended to consciously lower the quality of the Fender products and to some extent it attempted the contrary by trying to increase their standardization and consistency. To this end, a new 120,000 square foot building with modern equipment was erected in 1965 next to the existing FENDER premises to provide a better manufacturing environment. Problem is that it did not quite turn out right. So, what went wrong? First of all, CBS corporate bureaucracy and formal management style suddenly hit FENDER like a mountain storm and began to severely affect the Company's former procedures. The change in management style was resented by many employees, all the more as FREDDIE TAVARES recalls that: **«Actually, there was no prior mention to us down on the production line about the sale to CBS»**(51). It wasn't long before disputes broke out between CBS and some of the former senior managers of FENDER. For example, FORREST WHITE, who became

Jeff Beck and the Stratocaster, a perfect combination...

Blonde 1969

Jimi Hendrix, one of the all-time undisputed kings of the Stratocaster

Ry Cooder on stage with a bound neck mid-60's Stratocaster (courtesy Warner Bros.)

director of manufacturing in 1965, left in December 1967 after a bitter argument over production methods. Both LEO FENDER and DON RANDALL had a 5-year contract with CBS and were initially committed to stay to ensure the smooth continuity of the Company. DON RANDALL had been appointed general manager of FENDER MUSICAL INSTRUMENTS, but he did not last five years and he finally left in April 1969. LEO FENDER soldiered on, but according to FREDDIE TAVARES : **« Leo was hired by CBS as a consultant for 5 years, and at the end of the 5 years he didn't want anything to do with them anymore. In fact, at the end of the first year, he didn't want anything to do with them anymore ! »** (52).

Outside any emotional issue - let's not forget that all this is actually a business ! - quality problems mainly occurred because of CBS' major objective to boost output and productivity. Again, FREDDIE TAVARES vividly remembers : **« We had turned into a big fancy corporation all of sudden, where all the different departments had got their say in everything and then that was budgets, quotas and so on. They would try to put out the stuff as fast as they could !** (53). According to DON RANDALL, production was indeed increased by 45 % during the first year of operation of the new plant. It should be noted that at the time of the take-over FENDER had huge backorders on several models like the new Mustang and obviously CBS didn't want such a situation to continue when there was so much money at stake. FREDDIE TAVARES, who stayed at FENDER until he retired in 1986, puts it quite bluntly : **« When they [CBS] bought the Fender Company, they found out how profitable this operation was and they wanted the profits held right there. Like so many other American companies, it was to make sure the stockholders got plenty of dividends. So, what could the people around the plant do ? »** (54).

Meanwhile, CBS proceeded to patent some well-known FENDER trademarks such as the word « STRATOCASTER » or the ubiquitous backward Fender « F », now stamped on the neckplate and the tuning keys. Requests were filed on April 28,1967 and both trademarks were registered with the U.S. Patent Office on December 5,1967. About a decade later, the word « STRAT » was also filed by CBS on June 28,1976 and registered on February 8,1977.

The Stratocaster was not that popular in the mid-1960's as evidenced by its position in the Fender catalogues. At that time, it was not considered as a suitable instrument by many players under the influence of the British blues boom and power groups like CREAM, which usually relied upon a fatter Gibson type of sound. Production of the guitar reached a low ebb in 1967 which, in the author's experience, is probably the least abundant vintage in the 1960's. It took a young man by the name of JAMES MARSHALL HENDRIX to give the Stratocaster its second wind. The JIMI HENDRIX EXPERIENCE was formed in England in late 1966 and in early 1967 the group was achieving rock stardom, thanks to the blazing single « Hey Joe ». Jimi made a triumphant return to the U.S.A. in June 1967 when he stole the show at the Monterey Pop Festival, playing a Stratocaster in ways unheard of so far.

Because of his profound influence over many players - including some respected guitar heroes ! - JIMI HENDRIX was essential in (re)establishing the Stratocaster credentials. His preference for the Strat produced an immediate effect and helped the model to resume its leadership in the field of electric guitars.

Besides JIMI HENDRIX, other guitarists also contributed to the resurgence of the Stratocaster. Among them GEORGE HARRISON, who first used a Strat on the BEATLES' single 'Nowhere Man' released in early 1966 but gave it visible exposure during the 'Magical Mystery Tour' in 1967 or at the Concert For Bangla Desh in August 1971. In 1969, DAVID GILMOUR of PINK FLOYD was setting the controls for the heart of the sun with a Stratocaster and by 1970 famed virtuosos like ERIC CLAPTON or RITCHIE BLACKMORE from DEEP PURPLE had surrendered their Gibsons and opted for the Stratocaster.

1971 - 1981

The fourth period in the Stratocaster story could be subtitled **« CBS WITH A TILT NECK »** with reference to the neck adjusting system fitted to the model in 1971. During his 5-year tenure as a consultant with CBS/FENDER, LEO FENDER - who incidentally was cured of his strep

infection in 1967 - did some R § D. In 1970 he came up with a new device which he called **« tiltable guitar neck incorporating thrust absorbing pivot and locking element »**. Until then, truss rod adjustment on Fender instruments was carried out at the heel of the neck and correct neck pitch was achieved by inserting little shims in the neck pocket. The purpose of Leo's invention was to make life easier for players and to this end, truss rod adjustment was henceforth achieved by a « bullet » above the nut while pitch was set-up with the help of a small Allen screw located in the neck plate.

The patent of what became known as the « Tilt Neck » (for short) was registered on December 29,1970 and the new device was first fitted to the Stratocaster after mid-1971. It became a major feature, yet often disparaged, on the guitar and as such it embodies a distinct period in the Stratocaster story. Between mid-1971 and mid-1981, the basic appointments of the standard Stratocaster can be summarized as follows : (NB : * shows a change compared to the previous period).

1   two-piece neck with a 21-fret rosewood fretboard glued over maple OR one-piece Maple Neck.
2   « large » headstock.
3   black Fender logo.
4   chrome-plated Fender tuning keys with « F » stamped on back cover.
5 *   3-bolt neck mounting with built-in Tilt Neck adjustment.
6 *   truss rod adjustment with a « bullet » above the nut.
7 *   one-piece die-cast vibrato tailblock.
8 *   die-cast chrome-plated bridge saddles.
9 *   triple ply pickguard with 11 mounting screws and a white top until 1975, then with a black top.
10 *   3 single coil pickups with staggered polepieces until late 1974, then with flush polepieces.
11 *   faintly comfort- contoured ash body.
12   glossy polyester finish.

The « Tilt Neck » micro adjustement is not a bad idea, but at the end of the day it gradually brought a poor reputation to the 1970's Stratocasters because of its 3-bolt neck mounting system. By and large, guitar players are a rather conservative population of musicians and removing one bolt off the neck plate soon engendered suspicion of a less efficient neck joint. Such an assertion is probably debatable, but in conjunction with other changes carried out on the Stratocaster since 1965, it definitively enforced the « PRE- CBS » anthem among Fender afficionados.

This modern schism grew even stronger when other older features were discontinued in the course of the 1970's. For instance, the 2-piece vibrato block with a screwed-on inertia block was dropped in late 1971 and replaced by a one-piece die-cast unit with a heavy chrome plating. At the same time, the original steel saddles were also discarded in favour of solid die-cast units. By the end of 1974, the staggered polepieces were withdrawn from the pickups and replaced by flush poles. The non-adjustable polepieces were initially staggered to take into account the different string gauges at a time when most players were using fairly heavy sets. In the early 1970's, lighter sets with an unwound G string became the usual norm and instead of changing the size of the staggered poles, Fender opted for all-purpose flush poles. In 1975, a 3-ply black pickguard was first made available, while the model still retained white knobs and pickup covers. By 1976, the Stratocaster was fitted with an all black trim, since black was then considered « the choice of professional musicians throughout the international music world » as per FENDER contemporary brochures.

A 5-position selector switch was introduced in 1977 as a standard feature to enhance the sound selection, but this wasn't really a « first » as the so-called 'out of phase' sounds - so far obtained by carefully positioning the switch between the 3 regular slots - were long time favourites with guitar players. Besides, several part makers and suppliers were already listing 5-position replacement switches when FENDER finally jumped the bandwagon.

However, besides the « Tilt Neck », the most legitimate argument about the rather poor quality of the 1970's Stratocasters was brought about by the body and its finish. With the introduction of a « natural » finish in 1972, ash was gradually reinstated as the basic material for the body. Ash is a pretty inconsistent timber in terms of density and its weight can vary

Ritchie Blackmore on stage with a 70's "Tilt-necked" Stratocaster (courtesy Fender Musical Instruments)

The Anniversary : 25 years after...

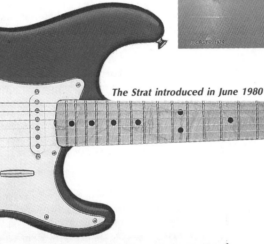

The Strat introduced in June 1980

1977 Stratocasters

Stevie Ray Vaughan playing one of the rare "Hendrix" Stratocasters, easily identified thanks to its reverse headstock (courtesy Alan Rogan)

to a 'arge extent. As a rule, the 1970's ash-bodied Stratocasters are heavier than most other Strats and, contrary to popular belief, this doesn't help with the sound or the sustaining capacity of the instrument. Due to a drastic increase in production output - by the late 1970's the Fullerton plant was producing some 480 guitars per day ! - workers on the line could not maintain the same attention to details and it soon reflected in the sculptured shape of the body. The lack of quality control is particularly conspicuous in the contours which were visibly reduced during the 1970's and became quite faint compared to a 1950's guitar. Pictures clearly illustrate the poorly contoured body of the 1970's instruments.

Mid-way through the decade, FENDER came up with its «Thick-Skin» high-gloss finish, which did nothing but enhance the 'plasticky' looks of its instruments. As implied by its registered designation, «Thick-Skin» meant that guitars were suddenly sprayed with 10 to 15 coats of an all-polyester finish! A few years later, FENDER was asked by both the Air Quality Management District (A.Q.M.D.) and the Environmental Protection Agency (E.P.A.) to modify its spraying installation and to find a less polluting finishing method. The Company then decided to try water-based finishes, which could be electrostatically sprayed on bodies. The new set-up was first used in 1979, but it soon turned into a disaster as finishes were prone to cracking and falling off after a couple of weeks or months! Needless to say that this unfortunate problem brought up quite a few claims from dealers and customers and ultimately cost FENDER a lot of money and caused a return to polyester finishes. Finally, throughout the 1970's the Company kept on restricting its custom colour selection and, for instance, only 6 finishes (including sunburst) were available between 1974 and 1977. A completely revised custom colour chart known as «the international colours» was later released but it proved to be so ugly that it only lasted for less than a year before being dropped in the course of 1981.

Without being overly detrimental to FENDER, there is no doubt that the Stratocasters produced during the 1970's helped to foster the craze for pre-CBS « vintage » guitars. Nevertheless, the Fullerton plant kept on churning out tons of Stratocasters (and other models) thanks to the increasing demand from export markets. Actually, despite the average quality of the Stratocasters of the decade, the 1971-1981 years saw an incredible rise to fame of the instrument, adopted by a growing number of players. Countless artists chose the Stratocaster as their workingman's axe... JEFF BECK, ROBBIE ROBERTSON (the Band), JJ CALE, RY COODER, FRANK ZAPPA, LOWELL GEORGE (Little Feat), RICHARD THOMPSON (Pentangle), NILS LOFGREN, RON WOOD (Rolling Stones), STEVE LUKATHER (Toto), etc. just to name a very few, not to mention mega stars like ERIC CLAPTON or BOB DYLAN. A new band called DIRE STRAITS also made an instant impact on the public in 1978, thanks to the talent and the Stratocaster sound of its leader MARK KNOPFLER. It should be noted, however, that those artists often played 'older' Statocasters and not 'newer' ones. Such a situation didn't go totally unnoticed at CBS/FENDER, which sensed that something had to be done to fully take advantage of the incredible popularity of the Stratocaster. This is the reason why additional variants were devised in the late 1970's.

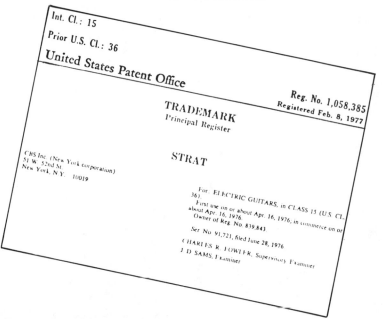

Int. Cl. : 15

Prior U.S. Cl. : 36

United States Patent Office

Reg. No. 1,058,385
Registered Feb. 8, 1977

TRADEMARK
Principal Register

CBS Inc. (New York corporation)
51 W. 52nd St.
New York, N.Y. 10019

STRAT

For ELECTRIC GUITARS, in CLASS 15 (U.S. Cl. 36).
First use on or about Apr. 16, 1976; in commerce on or about Apr. 16, 1976.
Owner of Reg. No. 839,843.

Ser. No. 91,721, filed June 28, 1976.

CHARLES R. FOWLER, Supervisory Examiner.
J D SAMS, Examiner.

THE ANNIVERSARY STRATOCASTER

Unveiled in June 1979 as a limited edition to celebrate the 25th anniversary of the model the ANNIVERSARY boasted a few specific features such as :
• a 4 bolt neck plate with the old style truss rod adjustment at the body end of the neck (in other words : no Tilt Neck !)
• deluxe Sperzel tuning keys with string post locking system.
• a 6-digit serial number, beginning with 25, stamped on the neckplate which also indicates « 1954 1979 - 25th ANNIVERSARY ».
• an exclusive silver metallic finish, with the commemorative designation of the model reproduced in black lettering on the upper horn of the body.

Actually, the earliest ANNIVERSARY guitars were sprayed with a near-white pearloid paint, as used by the Huffy Bicycle Company. Like most water-based finishes at that time, it often peeled and cracked and so the paint was dropped after an initial batch of ca.500 guitars. FENDER then opted for a silver metallic finish, made with Porsche automotive paint. The ANNIVERSARY was exclusively fitted with a one-piece Maple Neck and came with a « certificate of merit » logging the origin and the serial number of the instrument. According to FENDER, some 10,000 Anniversary Stratocasters were manufactured between 1979 and 1980.

THE STRAT

A year later, FENDER introduced at the NAMM show a customized and souped-up variant of the Stratocaster, simply called « THE STRAT » as per the long standing nickname of the guitar. Designed by GREGG WILSON, then chief of guitar R § D at FENDER with the help of DAN AMSTRONG as a consultant, THE STRAT aimed at blending a few classic features with modern electronics to rejuvenate the Stratocaster concept. As such it reinstated a smaller peghead, yet dissimilar to the original 1954-1965 design. Apparently, this mishap was caused by the absence of old blueprints and the re-design was done without actually checking out older guitars.

Like the Anniversary model, the new guitar was deprived of the Tilt Neck and fitted with the old style truss rod adjustment and 4-bolt neck plate. THE STRAT also incorporated some novel appointments such as :
• a hotter lead pickup (known as the X-1), with a stronger output than the standard Stratocaster unit.
• a new wiring circuitry delivering 9 different basic sounds.
• 22k gold electroplated brass hardware, including a re-designed extra massive bridge and vibrato block.

THE STRAT listed for $ 995 on June 15,1980 and could be ordered either with a rosewood fretboard or a one-piece Maple Neck. At first, it was exclusively available in two classic finishes : Candy Apple Red and Lake Placid Blue, with a painted-on headcap.
In the wake of the Strat, the STANDARD STRATOCASTER was also fitted with the hotter X-1 lead pickup June 1980, although for another year it retained its other 1970's features, such as the Tilt Neck or the large peghead. In 1980, FENDER also launched its « original brass works » accessories in order to seize some share in the then buoyant market of replacement parts and retrofitting hardware.

Finally, a third variant on the Stratocaster theme was also tentatively envisaged in 1980 at the request of MUDGE MILLER, then VP sales and Marketing at FENDER. Known today as the 'HENDRIX MODEL', this abortive variant was basically using the same construction as the ANNIVERSARY, except that it had a reverse headstock and an additional body contour on the front. According to FENDER, only 25 examples of this highly unusual Stratocaster were ever produced.

Both the ANNIVERSARY and THE STRAT sold quite well when they were introduced and, thanks to the magic of its name, the standard model remained a serious contender in the field of electrics despite its various shortcomings. However, although its MUSICAL INSTRUMENTS DIVISION - i.e. FENDER/ROGERS/RHODES/SQUIER-was still highly profitable in 1980 (NB : net sales of $ 60.5m with a pre-tax profit of $ 12.7m), CBS realized that it was steadily losing market share against other manufacturers.

This is why, in early 1981, CBS decided that it was time to « upgrade » FENDER and to put in more in tune with what was happening in the music industry.

1981 - 1985

The fifth period represents « CBS SWANSONG » and it was to mark the end of an era. In early 1981, CBS hired JOHN MCLAREN and BILL SCHULTZ from YAMAHA to take over the helm of its MUSICAL INSTRUMENTS DIVISION. Initial appraisals outlined several troublesome issues, which needed to be promptly addressed. For instance, a report dated May 19,1981 mentioned a « SHARP DECLINE IN PRODUCT QUALITY » and a « SIGNIFICANT INCREASE IN DOMESTIC AND FOREIGN DEALER COMPLAINTS ABOUT DEFECTIVE AND UNACCEPTABLE QUALITY ». The same report also outlined that the Company had followed a « POLICY OF HIGH MARGINS AND LITTLE PRODUCT IMPROVEMENT », allowing other manufacturers to enter the market with competitively priced, high quality products. Another confidential report dated May 30,1981 listed 9 major reasons for a decline in sales (NB : in May YTD FENDER sales were down 9 % compared to previous year), among which the most striking were the dealers' inability to realize a reasonable profit doing business with Fender, a poor product quality, the past policy of overpricing products, an inadequate after-sales support, etc. In a memo dated May 14,1981, ˋCHUCK VAN LIEW, director of manufacturing mentioned that **« With the exception of 1977, Fullerton has been on a program of restricted capital investment »** and he stressed the need for some substantial capital expenditure in order to purchase modern equipment for the plant. In other words : FENDER badly needed a shot in the arm !

Meanwhile, the 1981 Summer Convention was drawing near and in spite of its problems, FENDER had to show new products. Due to time constraints, it was not possible to completely revamp the standard Stratocaster and so it was decided to simply introduce two additional variants.

THE GOLD STRATOCASTER

The GOLD STRATOCASTER was a smart way to come up with something new, without retooling in any way. Announced in June 1981 as a limited edition in the Collector's Series, the model was basically a combination of parts featuring :
• THE STRAT body and one-piece Maple Neck with its (atrophied) smaller peghead
• the regular Stratocaster pickup assembly with a 3-ply white pickguard and white knobs.
• gold-plated brass hardware as offered in the standard 'Brassmaster Series' introduced in 1980.

Like THE STRAT, the GOLD STRATOCASTER was built without the large headstock and the micro Tilt Neck adjustment. It was exclusively available -hence its namesake- in a gold metallic finish (no painted-on headcap). According to FENDER, the hardware was actually plated with a 100 micron gold coat (same as fine jewelry) and for that reason it is rumoured that the Company lost money on every unit it sold ! This expensive detail also brought about its current nickname of « Gold-Gold Stratocaster ».

THE WALNUT STRAT

At the initiative of CHIP TODD-then chief R § D designer- FENDER also introduced in June 1981 a deluxe version of THE STRAT, entirely crafted of solid American Black Walnut. Known as The WALNUT STRAT (or sometimes Super Strat) the model was fitted with a one-piece walnut neck, black pickup covers and pickguard. Otherwise, its basic appointments were identical to The Strat, which at that time was made available in a 3rd finish, Artic White. THE WALNUT STRAT is an extremely good looking guitar, but because of its unique wood construction it is probably the heaviest Stratocaster ever built (along with its subsequent mate the Walnut Elite).

The standard Stratocaster did not undergo any structural modification for the 1981 Summer NAMM show and it was still fitted with the Micro Tilt Neck adjustment and the large peghead. Nevertheless, although it was still featured in one Fender ad (« people are the heart of the product ») during mid-to-late 1981, its days were counted !

In August 1981, DAN SMITH -who had been hired from Yamaha by Bill Schultz- came to FENDER as director of marketing and was asked to promptly develop a 5-year business plan for guitars. The new strategy, aimed at reviving sales, restoring quality control and extending the range of models, was presented in early September to THOMAS H. WYMAN, chairman and CEO of CBS Inc. The plan was okayed and as a consequence CBS agreed to spend some $ 2m on modernizing the Fullerton plant. The first decision of the new management team was then to actually drop full production from 250/300 guitars per day down to just a handful. DAN SMITH recalls : **« Basically our goal was initially to restore the confidence of the dealers and the players in Fender. The only way we could achieve that was to raise the quality levels back up ! We could not redesign the production line all at once so we started to initiate the steps to get the product back to where it hat to be, but while that was going on, we basically shut the plant down and retaught everybody how to make Fender guitars the way people wanted them. It took us probably 2 and a half years to achieve that ! »** (55).

The first two projects put together in late 1981 by DAN SMITH were the 'vintage re-issues' and the re-design of the standard Stratocaster.

THE VINTAGE REISSUES

On the threshold of the 1980's the craze for pre-CBS instruments had gathered momentum and an increasing number of players were keener on older guitars than on current models. DAN SMITH immediately perceived that FENDER should give people what they wanted and, with the help of JOHN PAGE, he proceeded to work on a reissue of the most popular designs of the Leo Fender era. Many old Strats from the 1950's and the early 1960's were thus closely studied and measured up in every respect to retrieve the true specifications of the original issues. In the process, well-known collectors such as LARRY HENRICKSON from DeKalb (Illinois) allowed Dan and John to scrutinize their collection. Amidst the varying specs of older instruments, two basic configurations were retained and developed into the '57 AND '62 VINTAGE STRATOCASTERS. Prototypes were completed in December 1981 and the two « new » models were officially introduced in January 1982 at the NAMM Convention in Anaheim.

FENDER backed its reissue programme with what is probably its most lavish ever catalogue (1982 « The sound that creates legend »), but the new models did not make it to the stores until much later. DAN SMITH explains : **« The facility was in such poor shape that we actually could not get into the manufacturing of the vintage guitars. We didn't deliver the Stratocaster reissues until near the end of 1982 »** (56).

Of course, as is often the case with reissues, it is possible for the stiff-necked connoisseur to quibble over the accuracy of certain details when comparing with originals. Actually, the Fender Vintage reissues should not be considered as genuine replicas of older guitars, but as their modern renditions. The rationale was to make available (and affordable) to a greater number of people a classic design with its basic appointments, bearing in mind contemporary requirements and/or constraints. For instance, neck profiles had to be standardized on both guitars and owing to players' overall preference, FENDER opted for a very flat cross-section unknown on any 1957 Stratocaster. Likewise, although the positioning of the 12th fret dots was correct on the prototypes (see 1982 catalogue pictures), this detail could not be duplicated on the production models because it would have entailed a costly retooling. This structural detail is probably the quickest way to spot a reissue at first sight from afar! Also, the '62 reissue does not feature the typical 'clay dots' nor the 'greenish' nitrate pickguard and there are no patent numbers on the headstock etc. The list could go on, but again it was not FENDER's intention to make perfect replicas of its older guitars. Incidentally, although the rosewood fretboard reissues (i.e. Stratocaster, P. Bass and J. Bass) were rather based on 1961 instruments, they were all given a '62 designation. According to DAN SMITH, this was done so that FENDER could retain the possibility to drop the «slab board» if necessary, without actually changing the catalogue references.

In late 1981, FENDER also revamped the regular Stratocaster and finally did away with its large headstock and Micro Tilt Neck adjustment. DAN SMITH reverted to the classic 4-bolt neck fastening and made sure that the small peghead was more accurate than on THE STRAT. Consequently, from December 1981 until 1983 the basic appointments of the new STANDARD STRATOCASTER (a.k.a. the « Smith Strat ») can be summarized as follows :
(NB :* shows a change compared to previous period)

1   two-piece neck with a 21-fret rosewood fretboard glued over maple OR one-piece Maple Neck.
2 *   « small » headstock.
3   black Fender logo.
4   chrome-plated Fender tuning keys with « F » stamped on back cover.
5 *   4-bolt neck mounting.
6 *   truss rod adjustment at the body end of the neck.
7   one-piece die-cast vibrato tailpiece.
8   chrome-plated die-cast bridge saddles.
9   triple ply white pickguard with 11 mounting screws.
10   3 single coil pickups with flush poles (inc. X-1 lead p.u.).
11 * deeply comfort-contoured alder body.
12 * polyurethane finish with polyester undercoat.

First listed in December 1981, the revised Standard Stratocaster was available in 6 standard and 7 new custom finishes, but owing to the Fullerton reshuffle it was not manufactured in very large quantities.

Besides the vintage and standard models, the 5-year business plan developed by DAN SMITH also featured three other significant issues for Fender guitars in general and the Stratocaster in particular. Only two of them materialized, but the third one, codenamed the 'ULTRA' series, never saw the light of day. The ULTRA STRATOCASTER was meant to feature neck-through-body construction, ebony fretboard, active electronics and rear-mounted components and as such it was poised to become the top of the Stratocaster line. The other two projects which did materialize were the ELITE series and the establishment of FENDER JAPAN.

THE ELITE STRATOCASTER

Work on the ELITE series commenced by Fall 1981 and involved a team of people consisting of DAN SMITH, CHIP TODD, JOHN PAGE, CHARLIE GRESSETT and... FREDDIE TAVARES (still going strong!). It was then an ambitious attempt to blend tradition with modern technologies and as such its prime objectives were to upgrade the electronics, the vibrato system and the neck adjustment. EMG was initially supposed to develop new circuits for FENDER, but could not be finalized. In order to avoid further delay in the release of the model, the active electronics of the ELITE guitars were eventually designed in a cooperative effort between ROGER COX, PAUL GUEGAN and BOB EGGLER. JOHN PAGE devised the refined Freeflyte tremolo/bridge section with drop-in string loading. CHARLIE GRESSETT came up with the Biflex truss rod, which makes it possible to adjust the neck curvature in two directions, convex and concave. After months of research and hard work, the ELITE STRATOCASTER was finally announced in May 1983 and compared to the existing variants of the Stratocaster it was built with no less than 16 novel features:
1 the Biflex truss rod adjustment
2 a neck angle adjuster located in the neck plate
3 a slightly wider nut width (1.700″)
4 a flatter fretboard radius (12″)
5 Ezy-Glyder point contact string retainers
6 high-ratio, lash free, specially lubricated tuning gears
7 security lock strap buttons
8 a heavy duty cast bridge assembly with 'drop-in' string loading
9 Freeflyte tremolo system with tension adjustable from the top
10 snap-on Torq-Master tremolo arm
11 Alnico II single coil pickups without protruding poles
12 noise-cancelling pickup system with a dummy coil between the lead and the middle pickups
13 active electronics with a special preamp circuitry including MDX (mid-range) and TBX (high-range) controls
14 three separate pickup push-push/on-off switches
15 an edge-mounted jack output
16 control knobs with a serrated rubber insert
Whereas some of these features could be viewed as refinements of existing concepts, the major departure from the usual FENDER ethics was undoubtedly the advent of active electronics. Their purpose was to offer a wider range of tones and the quietness of humbucking pickups, while retaining the brilliant single coil attack Fender guitars are associated with. In many respects, the ELITE SERIES certainly outlined the renewed innovating capacities of FENDER, but in an otherwise fairly conservative guitar world it did not prove a milestone as anticipated.

By mid-1983, the new model was released in 3 configurations :
• the ELITE STRATOCASTER, with heavy chrome-plated hardware, available with a rosewood fretboard or a one-piece Maple Neck in 6 standard finishes and 9 custom finishes
• the GOLD ELITE STRATOCASTER, same as above except gold electroplated hardware and pearloid buttons on tuners
• the WALNUT ELITE STRATOCASTER, with body and neck crafted from solid American Black Walnut, ebony fretboard, gold-electroplated hardware and pearloid buttons on tuners

Whatever the choice of fretboard (rosewood, maple or ebony), it should be noted that the neck was sporting a contrasting « skunk stripe » on its back, indicating that the Biflex truss rod was installed from the rear. The Elite body was also characterized by the absence of back recess (and back plate) for the tremolo springs and the small backplate near the edge covered the 9-volt battery required by the active circuitry.
With the introduction of the Elite series, THE STRAT, THE WALNUT STRAT and the GOLD STRATOCASTER were all dropped from the Fender price list of July 1, 1983.

Some of the innovative features of the Elite found their way onto the regular Stratocaster, which was again revamped in mid-1983. Between June 1983 and December 1984, the basic appointments of the STANDARD STRATOCASTER -whose list price had been lowered by some $ 295 over 6 months !- can be summarized as follows :
(NB : * shows changes compared to previous period).

1   two-piece neck with a 21 fret rosewood fretboard glued over maple OR one-piece Maple Neck.
2   «small» headstock.
3 *   silver «modern» Fender logo.
4 *   chrome-plated die-cast tuning keys with a Fender stamp on the back.
5   4-bolt neck mounting.
6 *   truss rod adjustment above the nut («Biflex»).
7 *   one-piece die-cast vibrato tailpiece with drop-in string loading and 'Freeflyte' tremolo system.
8 *   elongated chrome-plated die-cast bridge saddles.
9 *   single ply white pickguard with 12 mounting screws.
10   3 single coil pickups with flush polepieces.
11 * comfort-contoured alder body (without vibrato back cavity).
12   polyurethane finish with polyester undercoat.

The new Standard model also incorporated the neck-pitch adjuster, the flatter neck radius, the wider nut, safety-lock strap buttons and snap-on tremolo arm. Cosmetically speaking, however, its most discriminating features vis-à-vis the previous standard versions were a top-mounted jack output and a single tone control. At first, the guitar was exclusively available with a one-piece Maple Neck, but by popular request the rosewood fretboard version was again listed in January 1984. The choice of standard finishes was restricted to only four colours (Black, Sienna S/B, Brown S/B and Ivory) without any custom option. In late 1984 though, FENDER came up with its limited edition « marble » finishes (a.k.a. « bowling ball » finishes) and ca.225 Standard Stratocasters were delivered in « marblized » red, blue and gold colours (with assorted matching tee shirt !). Actually, this was bound to be the model's colourful swansong since the STANDARD STRATOCASTER (made in U.S.A.) was removed from the Fender catalogue in January 1985.

FENDER JAPAN CO. LTD

Although this book does not intend to deal with the numerous Fender guitars made in Japan (or in Korea) since the early 1980's, it would not present a fair view of the FENDER strategy without a few words about FENDER JAPAN Co Ltd. During the late 1970's, the Compagny saw its business increasingly affected by the countless copies and clones of its models manufactured in Japan and elsewhere. When DAN SMITH put together his business plan, he stressed the need for budget models aimed at fencing off imitators as well as at recapturing part of the lower end of the market. It was soon resolved, however, that the prevailing environment in the U.S.A. was not appropriate for such a project. Therefore, the obvious solution was then to opt for « offshore production » in Japan.

FENDER VINTAGE '57 STRATOCASTER
(P/N 100908)

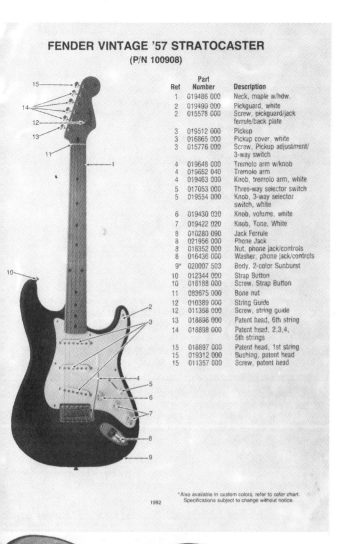

Ref	Part Number	Description
1	019486 000	Neck, maple w/hdw.
2	019490 000	Pickguard, white
2	015578 000	Screw, pickguard/jack ferrule/back plate
3	019512 000	Pickup
3	016865 000	Pickup cover, white
3	015776 000	Screw, Pickup adjustment/ 3-way switch
4	019648 000	Tremolo arm w/knob
4	019652 040	Tremolo arm
4	019463 000	Knob, tremolo arm, white
5	017053 000	Three-way selector switch
5	019554 000	Knob, 3-way selector switch, white
6	019430 030	Knob, volume, white
7	019422 020	Knob, Tone, White
8	010280 090	Jack Ferrule
8	021956 000	Phone Jack
8	016352 000	Nut, phone jack/controls
8	016436 000	Washer, phone jack/controls
9*	020007 503	Body, 2-color Sunburst
10	012344 000	Strap Button
10	016188 000	Screw, Strap Button
11	083675 000	Bone nut
12	010389 000	String Guide
12	011358 000	Screw, string guide
13	018896 000	Patent head, 6th string
14	018898 000	Patent head, 2,3,4, 5th strings
15	018897 000	Patent head, 1st string
15	019312 000	Bushing, patent head
15	011357 000	Screw, patent head

*Also available in custom colors, refer to color chart.
Specifications subject to change without notice.

1982

David Gilmour on stage with a '57 Vintage Reissue

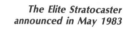

The Elite Stratocaster announced in May 1983

The Walnut Strat

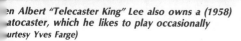

en Albert "Telecaster King" Lee also owns a (1958)
atocaster, which he likes to play occasionally
urtesy Yves Farge)

Jimmie Vaughan (Fabulous Thunderbirds) playing the Blues on a Stratocaster

Negotiations between CBS/FENDER and Japanese companies KANDA SHOKAI Corp. and YAMANO MUSIC Co Ltd (Fender distributors in Japan) began in December 1981. Less than three months later, the parties involved came to an agreement and FENDER JAPAN Co. Ltd was officially established on March 11,1982 as an American-Japanese joint venture with equal partners from each country. The agreement provided that Fender guitars made in Japan would be manufactured by FUJI GEN-GAKKI Mfg.Co., Ltd with designs and parts supplied by CBS/FENDER, while their distribution on the Japanese domestic market would be assumed by both KANDA SHOKAI and YAMANO MUSIC. It was also agreed that CBS/FENDER would have the final say in selecting the export territories for the Japanese Fender products.

The first product announcement took place on May 7,1982 at the Hotel Grand Palace in Tokyo where FENDER JAPAN displayed its own renditions of the 6 Vintage Reissues, albeit in more abundant variants to cater for the specific price segmentation of the Japanese market. These models - with a regular Fender logo and a tiny label 'made in Japan' underneath - were partly sold in Japan (2 000 units per month), but also exported to Europe (1 500 units per month)at the initiative of CBS/FENDER. This soon created some confusion and a conflicting situation arose with the same, but more expensive models from the U.S.A. DAN SMITH remembers : « **Some distributors felt that it could hurt the sales of American guitars, so we decided to use the 'Squier' brandname, a brandname that Fender owned** » (57). On October 13,1982 the SQUIER brandname, which belonged to FENDER MUSICAL INSTRUMENTS was officially introduced on guitars at the first FENDER JAPAN sales conference held in Tokyo. On the same day, BILL SCHULTZ also reaffirmed : « **We are now prepared to take positive measures to eliminate the dead copies. We will take legal measures against them... CBS will not allow the copy instruments** » (58). It was then decided that Japanese made Fender guitars should be confined to Japan and only Squier guitars should be sold overseas. However, none of the FENDER JAPAN products was then meant to be sold in the U.S.A. as indicated by DAN SMITH : « **In late 1981, when we first started with the Japanese, it was not meant for sale in the US, it was meant to be able to continue to have a share in the export markets. Finally, in 1983, we felt that we had to bring these guitars into the USA to be able to compete with other people that were taking our business. We tried everything we could to see if we could produce guitars in the US for below $ 500 and this was just not possible !** » (59). The stronger value of the Dollar prompted CBS/FENDER to realize that it needed agressively priced items to compete against foreign manufacturers on its home market. By Fall 1983, SQUIER guitars made in Japan started to be imported in America, where they became an instant success.

The first SQUIER STRATOCASTER available in the U.S.A. was basically a '72 model, with large headstock, 3-bolt neck and Micro Tilt Neck adjustment and in DAN SMITH's own words : « **It didn't have any features likely to interfere with the sale of American models** » (60). The guitar first appeared in the January 1,1984 price list, but it was already on the U.S. market a few months before. The reason behind this change of policy was crystal clear : the Japanese model listed for $ 369 (less case) when the US Standard Stratocaster went for $ 699 (with case). From this moment on, the Japanese Fenders would be sold around the world, including the U.S.A.

The CBS/FENDER « offshore » strategy may be open to criticism in the eyes of those who believe that a genuine Fender instrument has to be made in California, or at least in the U.S.A. Nevertheless, beyond any argument, it probably saved FENDER in 1985 once CBS proceeded to « pull the plug ». Despite a spate of improvements since 1981, FENDER was having trouble to effectively show a turnaround in profits and CBS cited red ink in its MUSICAL INSTRUMENTS DIVISION as part of the Company's poor interim results in 1984. At a meeting in New York in July 1984, BILL SCHULTZ was informed by CBS that FENDER was going to be put up for sale on the open market.

A few serious corporate buyers, such as Kaman Corp. or I.M.C., were the first to bid, but in November 1984 CBS also accepted the principle of a Management Buy-Out. Finally, after weeks of rumours and speculations, a statement released on the opening day (Feb.1st) of the 1985 NAMM Winter Convention marked the end of an era : « **CBS Inc. announced it has agreed in principle to sell Fender Musical Instruments, a unit of CBS Inc., to an investor group led by William Schultz, President of Fender Musical Instruments, for an undisclosed price. A definite agreement is currently being finalized and a signing is expected shortly** ». Both parties

entered into a contract on February 8,1985 and the sale was completed on March 12,1985. The 'investor group' actually consisted of ca.10 Fender employees (from the upper management), a local bank (FootHill Savings § Loans), a Chicago-based investment firm (Mesirow) and a prominent musician ! (NB : rumour has it that it would be Tommy Tedesco).

After 20 years of 'PRE-CBS' semantics, the 'POST-CBS' nomenclature was open !

1985 - 1993

When the agreement with CBS was announced, BILL SCHULTZ made it clear that : « **Contrary to some rumours, Fender products will continue to be made in the US, as well as in other countries** ». The question then was 'where in the US ?', because the huge Fullerton facility was not included in the agreement as explained by DAN SMITH : « **Because of the nature of the business at that time and the amount of money that we could raise, we didn't buy the land and the buildings that CBS also owned. The Fullerton building we were in was approximately 250,000 to 300,000 sq.ft...it was a very large plant and it was beyond the size of what we needed for how we planned to do business** » (61). Back in early 1985, the Dollar was stronger than ever and it had reached unprecedented peak points, against most currencies. This simply meant that US-made products were (on the whole) hardly competitive in terms of pricing.

Fullerton closed in 1985 and production of Fender guitars was then (temporarily) suspended in the U.S.A. By June, the independently-owned FENDER MUSICAL INSTRUMENTS Corp. (« F.M.I. ») moved its corporate headquarters to Brea and over Summer the Company found the premises it needed for its new manufacturing facility in the city of Corona (off the Riverside fwy). DAN SMITH remembers : « **It took us about 8 to 10 months to be able to set up the new factory. In October of 1985, we were finally able to open the doors for the guitar factory again** » (62). NO Fender guitars were made in the U.S.A. between February and October 1985 and during that period, F.M.I. relied upon FENDER JAPAN products, such as the CONTEMPORARY STRATOCASTER as well as inventories purchased from CBS. These Japanese guitars pretty much allowed the Compagny to survive until it was in a position to put its own act together, as indicated by DAN SMITH : « **When we decided we were going to make an attempt to buy the Company, I took a trip to Japan and worked very closely with Fuji Gen-Gakki to develop a new line of electric guitars for Fender. That allowed us to go to the trade show in early 1985 with 21 new models... those models got us going... those Japanese Strats bought us time !** » (63). By the end of 1985, F.M.I. was again able to supply US-made guitars.

Production in Corona began in October 1985 with only 10 people on the floor and the initial output of the new plant was thus limited to 5 guitars a day. By comparison, Fullerton was employing around 135 people and putting out some 200 guitars a day in July 1984 ! With such a restricted set-up, F.M.I. could not carry too many US models in its catalogue and it was resolved to retain only the Vintage Reissues. The '57 and '62 STRATOCASTERS were the first guitars on the line in Corona as they had constantly been the best selling items in the Vintage Series. The first two guitars actually produced in Corona were a pair of '57 models, finished in Fiesta Red. The first one (S/N V000001) is now treasured by BILL SCHULTZ, while the second one (S/N V000002) was presented to British guitarist HANK MARVIN at a special banquet in London on February 12,1986.

At the January 1986 NAMM Convention, a new model called the VINTAGE PLUS was first shown and listed. It was basically a Vintage Reissue fitted with updated Elite electronics (new circuitry with 12 dB boost) and a System III tremolo unit. Only two prototypes were made for the Convention and the model never made it to the production line. Although it was still listed in June 1986(?), Fender changed its mind and the VINTAGE PLUS was put on the backburner. Market conditions were changing and the Dollar was now showing a downward trend, so F.M.I. decided to embark on a bigger project, which could firmly anchor the production of guitars in the U.S.A. This project was the AMERICAN STANDARD.

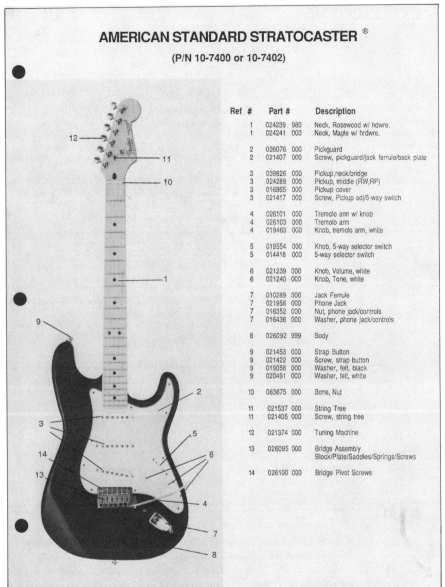

AMERICAN STANDARD STRATOCASTER ®

(P/N 10-7400 or 10-7402)

Ref #	Part #		Description
1	024239	980	Neck, Rosewood w/ hdwre.
1	024241	000	Neck, Maple w/ hrdwre.
2	026076	000	Pickguard
2	021407	000	Screw, pickguard/jack ferrule/back plate
3	039826	000	Pickup, neck/bridge
3	024288	000	Pickup, middle (RW,RP)
3	016865	000	Pickup cover
3	021417	000	Screw, Pickup adj/5-way switch
4	026101	000	Tremolo arm w/ knob
4	026103	000	Tremolo arm
4	019463	000	Knob, tremolo arm, white
5	019554	000	Knob, 5-way selector switch
5	014418	000	5-way selector switch
6	021239	000	Knob, Volume, white
6	021240	000	Knob, Tone, white
7	010289	000	Jack Ferrule
7	021956	000	Phone Jack
7	016352	000	Nut, phone jack/controls
7	016436	000	Washer, phone jack/controls
8	026092	999	Body
9	021453	000	Strap Button
9	021422	000	Screw, strap button
9	019056	000	Washer, felt, black
9	020491	000	Washer, felt, white
10	083675	000	Bone, Nut
11	021537	000	String Tree
11	021405	000	Screw, string tree
12	021374	000	Tuning Machine
13	026095	000	Bridge Assembly Block/Plate/Saddles/Springs/Screws
14	026100	000	Bridge Pivot Screws

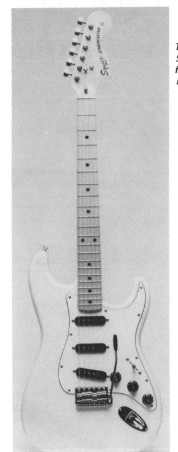

The Japanese-made Squier Stratocaster, first imported to the USA in late 1983

Robert Cray, at the forefront of a new generation of blues players

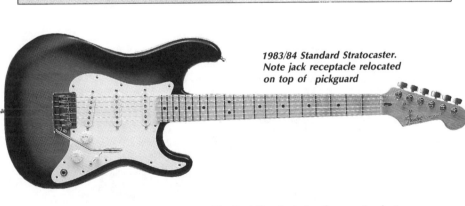

1983/84 Standard Stratocaster. Note jack receptacle relocated on top of pickguard

The Strat Plus, featuring the new Fender-Lace sensors

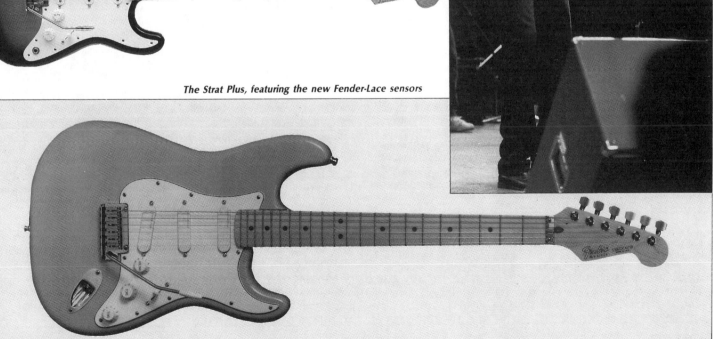

THE AMERICAN STANDARD

Thanks to a more favourable currency environment, the time was ripe for releasing a new U.S.-made standard Stratocaster. DAN SMITH sums up the rationale behind the new model: **"What we tried to do was to take a classic, vintage-style guitar. Make very few changes but changes that we felt would help the instrument, such as a better working tremolo, stainless steel saddles with 2 pivot posts and pickups with flat polepieces. Basically it was an upgraded vintage guitar"** (64). The development of the AMERICAN STANDARD—the designation was meant to reflect clearly the country of origin!—took place in mid-1986. The earliest samples were shipped in November 1986, but the model was officially unveiled at the January 1987 NAMM Convention with ERIC JOHNSON as its main endorser. The basic appointments of the new Standard can be summarized as follows:
(NB: *shows a change compared to the previous Standard model)

 1 * two-piece neck with a 22-fret rosewood fretboard glued over maple OR one-piece Maple Neck.
 2   "small headstock".
 3   silver "modern" logo.
 4   chrome-plated, die-cast tuning keys with a Fender stamp on the back cover.
 5   4-bolt neck mounting.
 6   truss-rod adjustment above the nut ("Biflex").
 7 * two-piece vibrato tailpiece with angled inertia block.
 8 * compressed stainless steel bridge saddles.
 9 * triple ply white pickguard with 11 mounting screws.
10   3 single-coil pickups with flush polepieces.
11   comfort-contoured alder body.
12   polyurethane finish.

The AMERICAN STANDARD has a truly out-of-phase middle pickup so that dual pickup combinations are in a noise-cancelling mode. For the first time, a US Stratocaster was fitted with 22 frets instead of 21 (NB: an upgraded version of the ELITE with 22 frets was scheduled in 1985). Otherwise, the model has an intermediate nut width (1.6815") and neck radius (9.5"), and it borrows a few features from the ELITE series like the Biflex truss-rod, the TBX tone control or Ezy-Glider string retainers.

Available in 6 finishes upon its introduction, the American Standard quickly became a world-wide success thanks to its extremely good value for money, and to the fact that it embodied a clever evolution of the classic Stratocaster design. The model also served as a stepping-stone, financially and otherwise, to develop a modern range of Stratocaster guitars. Indeed the ensuing years saw the inception of an impressive number of new designs which, for the sake of clarity, are presented hereafter by family rather than in strict chronological order. But first mention should be made of two innovations which have greatly influenced the recent course of events: the Fender-Lace sensors and the Custom Shop operation.

THE FENDER LACE SENSORS

The short-lived Elite model or the aborted Vintage Plus has shown that FENDER was keen to modernize the Stratocaster's pickups, albeit without radically altering their sound trademark. Back in 1983, a scientist by the name of DON LACE had approached DAN SMITH because he felt that the traditional electro-magnetic construction could be improved upon with modern technology. Don Lace (who passed away in late 1992) was at the head of ACTODYNE GENERAL, a California-based R&D firm with a wealth of experience in the field of magnetic and sensing devices. He sought to interest FENDER in novel pickup concepts, whereupon DAN SMITH gave him a specific brief: **"I said what really needs to be developed is a system that would allow somebody to sound like a Stratocaster, but not have any noise. To be honest, everything we tried that was humbucking supposedly single-coil replacement – whether stacked or blade side-by-side – did not sound like a Stratocaster! With a side-by-side coil relationship, you lose high-end response, and with a stacked coil, you usually lose bottom-end response"** (65).

Discussions with Don Lace were resumed after the CBS sale and a contract was eventually signed in September 1986 for the development of a whole range of new pickups for guitars and basses. A few more months proved necessary to carefully balance the sound of the earliest "sensor", so that it could replicate the late 50s Stratocaster sound while retaining its technical pluses over regular single-coil pickups. In early 1987 the first of the FENDER-LACE SENSORS, the Gold Strat, was ready to make its official début. Subsequently, other variants were developed so as to offer a choice of tonal response. The various FLS

are identified by their colour coding:

• Gold   = classic late 50s sounds
• Silver = punchier sound with more mid-range
• Blue   = clean late 50s humbucker sound
• Red   = high output humbucker sound

To enhance output and versatility in sound, FLS can also be combined in pair to form "dually's" which fit in the same-sized slot as a humbucking pickup. Of course, dual sensors only *resemble* humbuckers because of their side-by-side installation, but technically they are a totally different kettle of fish. In fact, the detailed characteristics of the FLS remain classified. Basically, they are passive units built with an intricate array of low energy particle magnets. The conventional polepieces are replaced by 36 micro comb teeth while the inner core is framed by metal sides (a.k.a. Radiant Field Barriers) to provide quietness of operation.

Whilst retaining a familiar quality of sounds, the radically innovative Lace sensors enabled F.M.I. to introduce a whole new generation of Stratocasters adequately blending classic and high-tech features.

THE CUSTOM SHOP

The inception of the first FLS coincided with the establishment of a CUSTOM DESIGN GUITAR & MANUFACTURING facility next to the Corona plant. Initially composed of two master builders, MICHAEL STEVENS and JOHN PAGE, its original brief was to build one-off superlative guitars for artists or trade show purposes, as well as "customized" parts for standard models. The success of the Custom Shop quickly exceeded all expectations, and its scope was extended to the production of limited edition models and custom guitars for the public. As a result, other experienced luthiers like JAY BLACK, LARRY BROOKS, JOHN ENGLISH, YASUHIKO IWANADE, FRED STUART gradually joined forces with Michael and John along with several apprentices. In 1990 the Fender R&D department was merged into the Custom Shop and JOHN PAGE was appointed manager of the combined operations. This smart move allowed seasoned R&D engineers like GEORGE BLANDA or STEVE BOULANGER to work in closer cooperation with what earned the well-deserved moniker of "dream factory".

The Custom Shop facility has played a key role in the design and production of new Fender models, particularly the SIGNATURE series. The only downside is that it has become practically impossible since 1987 to keep track of all Stratocaster variants in existence! Its prolific creations and re-creations would almost require a book of their own.

For the record, the first limited produced by the Custom Shop was a faithful rendition of Blonde '57 and '62 variants with gold parts, commonly nicknamed the "Mary Kaye" models by reference to the artist shown with that guitar in old Fender catalogues. A total of about 1,000 MARY KAYEs were made between mid-1987 and late 1989. The next run was a reissue of the tri-gold model (ie gold finish, gold parts and gold pickguard) made in the late 50s for Homer Haynes of the musical duo Homer & Jethro. Only 500 units of the HLE (ie Haynes Limited Edition) were built over 1989-1990 and specially numbered from 001 to 500. In 1989 the Shop was also entrusted with the task of designing and building the 35TH ANNIVERSARY STRATOCASTER. Loosely based on the Strat Plus (see below), the model boasts 3 Silver FLS, a dazzling quilted maple top and an ebony fretboard inlaid with abalone dots. Again, only 500 units of the 35th Anniversary Stratocaster were built between 1989 and 1991.

In addition to these "official" limited editions, the Custom Shop also makes smaller runs of special guitars at the request of Fender authorized dealers and sales reps. The CARSON STRATOCASTER or the TEXAS SPECIAL with its typically fat-sounding pickups illustrate this highly successful policy. The HARLEY DAVIDSON 90TH ANNIVERSARY Commemorative Stratocaster produced in 1993 (only 109 built) with an engraved aluminum body is per-haps to date the fanciest of them all! Instigated in late 1992, the CLASSIC SERIES offers faithful recreations of the '54 and '60 Stratocasters, as well as a Custom Shop version of the American Standard known as the AMERICAN CLASSIC STRAT.

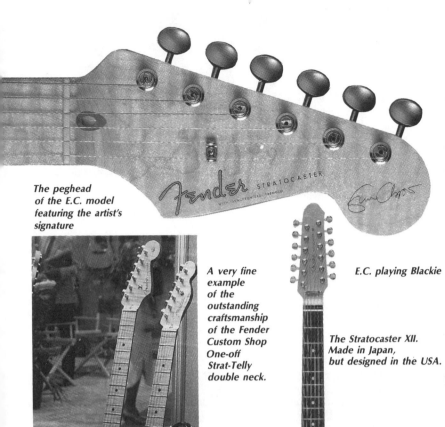

The peghead of the E.C. model featuring the artist's signature

A very fine example of the outstanding craftsmanship of the Fender Custom Shop One-off Strat-Telly double neck.

The Stratocaster XII. Made in Japan, but designed in the USA.

E.C. playing Blackie

Yngwie Malmsteen, a rising force in rock guitar (courtesy PolyGram Records)

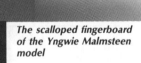

The scalloped fingerboard of the Yngwie Malmsteen model

THE PLUS SERIES

The STRAT PLUS was developed in the wake of the American Standard as the two models were initially poised to be introduced simultaneously. At the outset, the basic idea was to come up with an enhanced Stratocaster incorporating active electronics like the Vintage Plus prototype. But the project was altered in late 1986 so that the STRAT PLUS could be the first Fender instrument fitted with the new Gold Lace sensors. The model also served to premier the "roller-nut" designed by Englishman TREVOR WILKINSON to reduce friction at the nut when using the tremolo. Locking tuners (at first Sperzel, then Schaller) were added to prevent string slippage whilst conversely the traditional string retainers were abandoned. Otherwise, the STRAT PLUS shared the same basic specifications as the American Standard.

The model first appeared in print in the price list dated March 1, 1987, but its introduction was actually postponed by a few months, partly because of a short supply of certain components, partly for specific "marketing reasons". A few months earlier, JEFF BECK had asked Fender to make him a '62 Vintage model painted in the same yellow colour as the souped-up Ford truck featured in the movie American Graffiti. The company obliged but seized the opportunity to talk Jeff into having a namesake Stratocaster model. The STRAT PLUS prototype was therefore put together with Jeff Beck in mind, hence its yellow finish christened "Graffiti Yellow". But Beck (temporarily) turned down FENDER's proposal and the first Stratocaster with sensors came out as the STRAT PLUS.

The favourable response to the model (and to the new sensors) led F.M.I. to introduce the DELUXE STRAT PLUS in January 1989. The first version, produced for about a year, is identical to the regular Plus save for two Silver FLS in the neck and middle positions and a Blue FLS near the bridge. A year later a revamped Deluxe Plus was released with an alternative combination of sensors, ie Silver in neck position, Blue in middle position and Red in bridge position. To provide for a lighter weight the body was also modified with an alder core sandwiched by slabs of ash on the front and back. A DELUXE AMERICAN STANDARD outfitted with three Gold sensors was also introduced in January 1989, but it remained in production for only a year.

The ultimate exponent of the Plus series came out in January 1990 in the form of the STRAT ULTRA (the name had been in the can since the early 1980s!). Compared to the previous Plus models, the Ultra is primarily characterized by its electronics featuring no less than four sensors: a Blue FLS in the neck position, a Silver FLS in the middle position, and a super hot Dual Red in the bridge position. The latter is wired to a 3-position mini toggle switch acting as splitter which, combined with the main pickup selector, contributes to giving an unprecedented palette of sounds.

The STRAT ULTRA also pioneered a new Deluxe tremolo featuring a heavier snap-in arm (without plastic tip) and a device called the Hipshot Trem-Setter. This device, basically consisting of a finely adjustable tension spring, limits the bridge movement to tremolo usage and ensures a return to the exact balanced (zero) position. Upon the release of the Strat Ultra, the DELUXE STRAT PLUS was also fitted with the Hipshot Trem-Setter. Special care was naturally brought to the looks and the construction of the Ultra. The center-core alder body was thus capped on top and back with highly figured maple whilst the exclusive ebony fretboard was inlaid with abalone dot markers.

THE SIGNATURE SERIES

Calling a model after an artist was not exactly a fresh idea when F.M.I. set out to launch the Signature series. But as DAN SMITH aptly comments: **"Our desire with the whole Signature series was to build the guitars exactly the way the artists play them. We didn't just want to build something that everybody was going to buy and then the artist had to have his different"** (66). Prior to the CBS divestiture, a signature project had been envisaged with Telecaster virtuoso JAMES BURTON, but the honour to start the series eventually fell on guitar legend ERIC CLAPTON.

*THE ERIC CLAPTON MODEL

In 1985 E.C. realized that the neck of his beloved Blackie (his late 50s "composite" Stratocaster) could not take another refret. At a gig in Dallas, DAN SMITH managed to bring him two hard-tailed Elites for a try, but Eric specified his requirements for a V-neck and more "compression" sound-wise. The seeds for a Clapton model were sown. Two prototypes were subsequently built with selected V-necks and upgraded Elite electronics featuring a +12dB boost circuitry. Both guitars were presented to E.C. in Spring 1986, but Slow Hand kept on asking for more compression. This prompted Fender to replace the Elite pickups by Gold FLS which, combined with a new mid-range tone control, delivered a 21dB boost compared to the classic Stratocaster sound. The Eric Clapton model was born.

The contract between Eric Clapton and F.M.I. was signed on May 7, 1987, but the production of the model was delayed until Spring 1988. Structurally, the Clapton Stratocaster is a '57 Vintage reissue modified with a few specific appointments such as:

• 3 Gold FLS with active electronics
• a master TBX tone control and a mid-range boost control
• a slightly flatter 8.5" neck radius
• a blocked-off tremolo assembly

The original finishes available on the guitar were also chosen by E.C., ie Pewter (anthracite), Torino Red (a.k.a. Ferrari Red) and Candy Green (a.k.a. 7-UP Green). The earliest samples are characterized by a 21-fret vintage neck and a mini switch to select active/passive electronics. In a matter of months, though, the model received a 22-fret neck with a Biflex truss-rod, and the mode switch was deleted while the mid-range boost was increased to +25dB. As a distinctive trademark for the new series, the actual signature of the artist is reproduced on the headstock. To date the Clapton remains the best-selling Signature Stratocaster.

*THE YNGWIE MALMSTEEN MODEL

While the E.C. model was taking shape, discussions were initiated in 1986 with Swedish guitarist, Yngwie Malmsteen, for the production of a Signature model. An agreement was reached in early 1987 and the first prototypes were displayed at trade shows the same year, but the Y.M. model did not hit the production line until mid-1988.

The Malmsteen is loosely based on a '56 alder-bodied Stratocaster modified with the following appointments:

• two DiMarzio HBS-3 humbuckers (with stacked coils) in the neck and bridge positions.

• an American Standard pickup, almost flush with the pickguard, in the middle position.

• two TBX tone controls (neck p.u. and mid/bridge p.u. together).

• a scalloped fingerboard and a brass nut.

• an American Standard tremolo assembly

In addition to the US-made Signature model, a less expensive offshore variant called the Yngwie Malmsteen Standard Stratocaster also appeared in 1990. However, the two guitars cannot be confused because the latter is based on a 70s Stratocaster with large headstock.

*THE ROBERT CRAY MODEL

The next Signature Strat was expressly designed to meet the requirements of Robert Cray, a leading exponent of the younger generation of blues performers. Introduced in 1990, the Cray combines features of the '58 non-trem and the '64 Inca Silver Stratocasters originally used by the artist. The result is essentially a non-tremolo '64 Stratocaster fitted with custom-wound pickups for the bright and crisp tones associated with Robert's stinging guitar styles. The rosewood-capped neck has an "oval" shape whilst the electronics are upgraded with a 5-position switch. However, unlike the Clapton and the Malmsteen, the Robert Cray model is built to custom order only.

*THE JEFF BECK MODEL

When F.M.I. first approached him in early 1987 to lend his name to a Signature model, Jeff Beck replied that he was not sure he deserved it! He nonetheless adopted as his main instrument the Strat Plus that was meant to carry his signature. A few years later, Jeff changed his mind and agreed to design a Stratocaster that would give him all the ultimate appointments he needed.

The Beck Stratocaster was first announced in January 1990, but it did not come out until about a year later. It is essentially a Strat Plus outfitted with four Gold FLS, including a dually in bridge position. A push-button switch next to the tone controls permits the player to turn on the second bridge unit so as to produce a thicker sound. The early 50s style neck is tailored to Jeff's specifications and currently features a pao ferro fretboard instead of the rosewood fretboard of the earliest samples. The basic colours are Midnight Purple, Surf Green and Vintage White.

"The locking keys found on the Plus series models as well as on limited editions like the 35th Anniversary Stratocaster"

"The non-tremolo Robert Cray Signature model"

"Richie Sambora: the latest artist to date to have lent his name to a Signature Stratocaster" (photo by Larry Busacca)

"Far left: 1987 Alex Gregory Signature model with reverse peghead. The basic version normally features a standard peghead with the 7 tuners on the upper side. Left: US-made H.M. Strat with maple neck"

"The Set-Neck Stratocaster with four sensors and Deluxe American Standard tremolo assembly"

*THE STEVIE RAY VAUGHAN MODEL

Commissioned before Stevie's tragic death in a helicopter accident in 1990, the SRV model was officially unveiled in January 1992 as a tribute to this master of blues. It is a modern rendition of the beat-up '59 Stratocaster with a '62 neck that Stevie Ray Vaughan used throughout his career. As one would expect, it is based on a '62 Vintage reissue with 3-tone sunburst, modified with a few specific features such as:

- Texas Special fat-sounding pickups.
- a triple-ply black pickguard enhanced with white SRV initials.
- a left-handed vintage-style tremolo assembly.
- a 12" radius fretboard.
- gold-plated hardware.

Since its inception, the SRV has become a firm favourite in the Signature series.

*THE RICHIE SAMBORA MODEL

The Sambora Signature model is rooted in the custom HRR Stratocaster created for the artist by the Custom Shop in 1990. HRR stands for Hot Rodded Reissue and refers to the series of offshore-made Stratocasters marketed by F.M.I. since 1990. More generally, the HRR models belong to a new generation of Stratocasters equipped with a Gibson-style humbucker in the bridge position and a double-locking Floyd Rose tremolo system.

Introducing in 1993, the Sambora is basically an alder-bodied 50s Stratocaster fitted with the following appointments:

- 22-fret Maple Neck with star-shaped pearl inlays.
- a flatter 12" radius fretboard.
- a DiMarzio Pro PAF humbucker in bridge position.
- Texas Special single-coil pickups in neck and middle positions
- a TBX tone control for the middle and bridge pickups
- a double locking Floyd Rose tremolo.

The basic finish of the model is a vintage-style Arctic White, but cherry sunburst is also available.

In addition to these models, other Signature Stratocasters – characterized by the signature of the artist on the peghead – have been built by the Custom Shop, albeit on a limited scale. In 1987 an agreement was signed with English guitarist ALEX GREGORY for the production of a 7-string Stratocaster with an extended 24-fret range. Also known as the "Guitolin", this unusual model was designed, inter alia, to allow for the transposition to the guitar of Paganini's Caprices violin solos. Two prototypes were built in 1987 (one with a regular, the other with a reverse peghead), but subsequently the ALEX GREGORY MODEL was never listed among the available Stratocasters.

In 1990 the production of a limited run of a HANK MARVIN MODEL was commissioned by the Fender UK distributor. After some toing and froing regarding the final specs, the Marvin came out essentially as a late 50s style Stratocaster fitted with three FLS wired to an active circuitry, an American Standard tremolo and a black nut. Only 25 units were originally made in Fiesta Red with gold hardware, as per the mythical late 50s Stratocaster played by Hank with The Shadows. Beginning in 1992, however, a Japanese-made Hank Marvin Signature model marketed under the Squier brand. In 1992 the Custom Shop issued a DICK DALE MODEL, meant as a recreation of the surf king's 1960 Stratocaster and characterized by a gold sparkle finish, a reverse peghead and a reverse-angled bridge pickup.

FLOYD ROSE & HUMBUCKER

Since the mid-80s FENDER JAPAN had caught on with the wants and needs of younger players by releasing Stratocasters equipped with heavy-duty double-locking tremolo systems and Gibson-style humbucking pick-ups. In 1989 it was resolved to supplement the production of the US operation with such "rock-oriented" versions.

A US-made CONTEMPORARY STRATOCASTER was first listed in July 1989 and made for about two years. In addition to a Floyd Rose-licensed tremolo system and a DiMarzio humbucker in bridge position, the model was characterized by a figured maple top and back, a 22-fret rosewood fingerboard with 12" radius, and a master TBX tone control. In mid-1989 F.M.I. also released US-made versions of the H.M. Strat (H.M. stands for Heavy Metal), originally introduced in January 1988 as an offshore model. Available in various pickup configurations combining DiMarzio humbuckers, American Standard single-coils and FLS, the H.M. Strats are primarily characterized by a 24-fret neck, a black-painted headcap and a slightly smaller, more sharply contoured basswood body.

By mid-1990 the US-made H.M. Strats were phased out on the introduction of an upscaled variant called the H.M. STRAT ULTRA. As implied by its designation, the newer version shared some of the appointments of the Plus-series Strat Ultra, such as four FLS (including a dual red in bridge position), a body with a figured maple top and back, or an ebony fretboard. The H.M. Ultra remained cataloged for two years before being discontinued.

In January 1991 F.M.I. made the headlines by announcing that FLOYD ROSE, the inventor of the double-locking tremolo, had joined forces with the company. This smart move was the prelude to the introduction in 1992 of the FLOYD ROSE CLASSIC STRATOCASTER, meant as the right match between a traditional Stratocaster design and the modern tools of rock and roll. Available with a Maple Neck or a rosewood fretboard, the alder-bodied Floyd Rose Classic features:

- a DiMarzio PAF Pro humbucker in bridge position.
- two American Standard single-coil units in neck and middle positions.
- a 22-fret fingerboard with a 9.5" radius.
- vintage-style tuners and headstock logo.

and naturally a Floyd Rose tremolo system! A more affordable Squier variant, built in the new Ensenada factory in Mexico, was also marketed shortly after the release of the US model.

As if the spate of new models released since 1987 was not enough to consolidate the pre-eminent position of the Stratocaster among electric guitars, F.M.I. managed to expand farther its ambit with the advent of the Set-Neck models. In Spring 1990 a novel type of neck joint was developed by JOHN PAGE and STEVE BOULANGER so as to enable Fender to produce guitars with a glued-on neck, albeit without the constraints inherent to a classic dovetail joint. The process was first applied in Summer 1990 to a new breed of Telecaster models, thereby breaking with four decades of traditional bolted-neck construction.

The SET-NECK STRATOCASTER and SET-NECK FLOYD ROSE STRAT were put into production in late 1992 and premiered in January 1993. The two models feature a highly figured maple top and a 22-fret ebony fingerboard, but differ in their electronics and tremolo system. The Set-Neck Stratocaster has the same features as the Strat Ultra (ie 4 FLS and Deluxe Tremolo) whereas the Set-Neck Strat is outfitted with the pickups and hardware of the Floyd Rose Classic. Both guitars are built by the Custom Shop and may be considered as the ultimate exponents of the modern generation of Stratocasters.

Forty years after its inception, the Stratocaster has very few contenders to challenge its position as the most popular electric guitar. It is estimated that nearly 1,000,000 units have been produced in the USA since 1954, and in the last 10 years Stratocasters alone have accounted for more than 70% of all Fender guitar and bass sales. The creation of the late LEO FENDER has now become an industry standard, and many manufacturers have found it almost mandatory to produce an equivalent or at least a Strat-styled design.

After the intermezzo inherent to the CBS divestiture in 1985, the "new" Fender Musical Instruments Corporation has opened up a whole new chapter in the Stratocaster story. The unprecedented number of variants recently introduced bear testimony to the popularity of the instrument's timeless design, but also to the renewed creativity of Fender. In times when fashions and trends change at a frantic pace, the Stratocaster is ready to enter the third millennium. Meanwhile, players and collectors alike will no doubt seek to acquire one of the 1,954 examples of the special 40th Anniversary edition designed to commemorate four decades of success!

■ *CHAPTER NOTES* ■

Excerpts from conversations between Freddie Tavares and the author (January 1988) :
3+6+8+9+10+12+14+17+18+21+23+26+28+29+31+ 32+34+38+40+41+46+49+52+53+54

Excerpts from a conversation between Bill Carson and the author (January 1988) :
4+5+7+13+20+24+25+27+35+42+47+50

Excerpts from a conversation between George Fullerton and the author (January 1988) :
39+43+44+45+48

Excerpts from conversations between Dan Smith and the author (January 1988) :
55+56+57+59+60+61+62+63+64+65+66

Excerpts from a Klaus Blasquiz interview with Leo Fender, George Fullerton and Dale Hyatt published in DISC Magazine (1980) :
1+15+19+37

Excerpts from a Tom Wheeler interview with Leo Fender (and Freddie Tavares) published in Guitar Player Magazine (May 1978) :
2+11+30+51

Excerpts from a Tom Wheeler interview with Leo Fender published in Guitar Player Magazine (October 1979) :
16+22+36

Excerpts from a Ray Hammond interview with Leo Fender published in International Musician Magazine (March 1978) :
33

Excerpts from a report published in Japan Music Trades Magazine (December 1982) :
58

"Neck marking & serial number of one of the earliest 1954 production models"
(courtesy Perry Margouleff/Barry Hyman)

"Unusual 1956 example (#10268) with modifed layout for the controls, Telecaster-style metal knobs and black anodized pickguard. These experimental features can be traced back on at least one 1954 Stratocaster"

"1954 with original form-fit case"
(courtesy Patrice Bastien)

"Ultra rare May '56 example (#11531) with original metallic green finish"
(courtesy Didier Dodeman)

"1956 (#10388) with custom-ordered black finish. Who wants an original Blackie?"
(courtesy Didier Dodeman)

"1957 Blonde with gold hardware, commonly nicknamed the Mary Kaye Stratocaster" (courtesy Didier Dodeman)

"1959 with 3-tone sunburst" (courtesy Larry Henrickson/Dan Smith)

"Rare 1957 example (#-22178) in Shoreline Gold finish with gold parts" (courtesy Didier Dodeman)

"Back view of 1957 non-tremolo variant" (courtesy Philip Lang)

"A highly desirable 1957 model (#-19295) with the classic Fiesta Red finish" (courtesy Gérard Féraud)

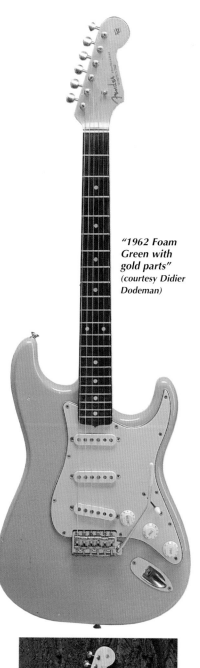

"1962 Foam Green with gold parts" (courtesy Didier Dodeman)

"7-59 rosewood board model. Note single-ply pickguard with 10 mounting screws" (courtesy Patrice Bastien)

"11-61 slab-board model with Sherwood Green metallic finish" (courtesy Didier Dodeman)

"1961 hardtail with early Fiesta Red shade, a.k.a. Coral Pink finish" (courtesy Philip Lang)

"1960 Blonde with gold parts"

"1964 Dakota Red (#L41824)."
(courtesy Gérard Féraud)

"Early 1963 sample with gold metallic finish"
(courtesy Didier Dodeman)

"1963 Olympic White with shell pickguard" (courtesy Didier Dodeman)

"1963 Daphne Blue"

"Back of 1963 model with Candy Apple Red finish" (courtesy Uncle Lou Gatanas)

"This 1968 maple-board model once belonged to Jimi Hendrix"
(courtesy M.M./photo Carleton)

"Top: 1965 Sonic Blue.   Above: 1965 Lake Placid Blue"
(courtesy Larry Henrickson/Dan Smith)

CUSTOM FINISHES FOR *Fender* FINE ELECTRIC INSTRUMENTS

These 14 Colors, plus Blond, Available at 5% Additional cost
Sunburst Finishes Standard at no Extra cost

LAKE PLACID BLUE METALLIC	OCEAN TURQUOISE METALLIC
2820-L	4607-L
BLUE ICE METALLIC	TEAL GREEN METALLIC
4692-L	4297-L
SONIC BLUE	
2095	
FIREMIST GOLD METALLIC	FOAM GREEN
4579-LH	209A
CHARCOAL FROST METALLIC	FIREMIST SILVER METALLIC
4583-L	4576-H
	CANDY APPLE RED METALLIC
OLYMPIC WHITE	DAKOTA RED
2810-L	2690-H
BLACK	FIESTA RED
1712-X	2210-H

Not available for Mustang, Duo-Sonic and Musicmaster
Colors Subject to Change Without Notice

"1966-67 custom colour chart"

"1965 Teal Green metallic"
(courtesy Perry Margouleff)

"The limited edition HENDRIX Stratocaster with reverse headstock and front contour" (courtesy Perry Margouleff/Barry Hyman)

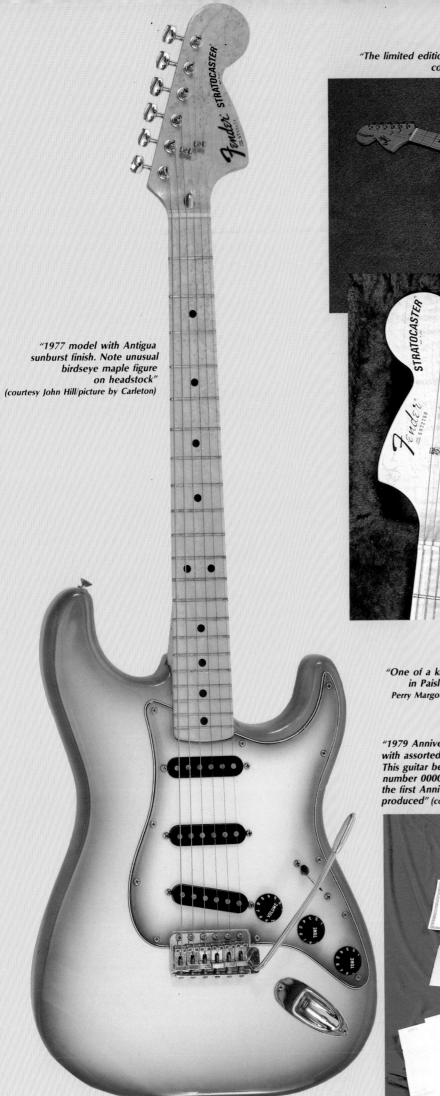

"1977 model with Antigua sunburst finish. Note unusual birdseye maple figure on headstock"
(courtesy John Hill/picture by Carleton)

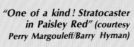

"One of a kind ! Stratocaster in Paisley Red" (courtesy Perry Margouleff/Barry Hyman)

"1979 Anniversary Stratocaster with assorted paraphernalia. This guitar bears serial number 000000 and was the first Anniversary ever produced" (courtesy John Sprung)

40

"1981 Gold/Gold Stratocaster with actual gold plating" (courtesy John Hill/picture by Carleton)

"1984 Standard Stratocaster with red marble finish"
(courtesy Steve Evans)

"The Strat in Artic White"

"1983 Gold Elite
in Candy Apple Green"

"62 Vintage Reissue"

"1982 regular model a.k.a.
Smith Stratocaster"

"The Strat Ultra: the ultimate model in the Plus series"

"American Standard: the first post-CBS design"

"1987 Strat Plus in Graffiti Yellow"

"57 Vintage Stratocaster in Fiesta Red. This particular instrument (#V000001) was the first guitar produced in Corona after the CBS sale"

"35th Anniversary model"

"Stevie Ray Vaughan Signature model"

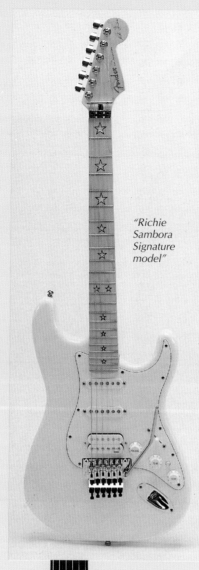

"Richie Sambora Signature model"

"Early production sample of the Eric Clapton model. Note 21-fret fingerboard and active/passive electronics mini-switch"

"Jeff Beck Signature model"

"Yngwie Malmsteen Signature model with scalloped fingerboard"

"Custom Classic 1960 (left) and 1954 (right)"

"Custom Shop model with dazzling quilted maple body and Tree of Life inlay on the fingerboard"

"Set-Neck Floyd Rose Strat with reverse peghead"

"The aluminum-bodied Harley Davidson 90th Anniversary model"

"1992 Floyd Rose Classic Stratocaster"

DATE	MODEL	PRICE	DATE	MODEL	PRICE	DATE	MODEL	PRICE
April 1954	tremolo	$249.50	**September 1979**	tremolo R/W	$750.00	**July 1989**	American Std (7)	$689.99
	non-tremolo	$229.50		tremolo M/N	$790.00		Deluxe American Std	$799.99
	+case $39.95			non-tremolo R/W	$695.00		Strat Plus	$899.99
				non-tremolo M/N	$740.00		Deluxe Strat Plus	$929.99
February 1957	tremolo	$274.50		25th Anniversary	$800.00		Vintage	$999.99
	Blonde/gold parts	$330.00		(6)			Mary Kaye Ltd Edition	$1199.99
	non-tremolo	$249.50					Clapton Signature	$1299.99
	+case $49.50		**September 1980**	tremolo (R/W or M/N)	$870.00		Malmsteen Signature	$1299.99
	(1)			non-tremolo			Contemporary	$799.99
				(R/W or M/N)	$815.00		H.M. Strat	$799.99
July 1960	tremolo	$289.50		The Strat	$995.00		(6)	
	custom finish	$303.97		(6) (7)				
	custom finish/gold parts	$349.50				**January 1990**	American Std (7)	$749.99
	non-tremolo	$259.50	**December 1981**	tremolo	$895.00		Start Plus	$899.99
	+case $52.50			non-tremolo	$840.00		Deluxe Strat Plus	$999.99
	(1) (2)			The Strat	$1095.00		Strat Ultra	$1399.99
				The Walnut Strat	$1195.00		Vintage	$1099.99
August 1965	tremolo	$281.00		Gold Stratocaster	$975.00		Clapton Signature	$1299.99
	custom finish	$295.00		Vintage	$945.00		Malmsteen Signature	$1299.99
	custom finish/gold parts	$337.00		(6) (7)			Beck Signature	TBA
	non-tremolo	$252.00					Contemporary	$849.99
	+case $52.50		**July 1983**	Std tremolo M/N	$650.00		H.M. Strat	$839.99
	(1) (2) (3)			Std non-tremolo M/N	$585.00		H.M. Strat Ultra	$1449.99
				Vintage	$995.00		(6)	
October 1966	tremolo	$299.50		Elite	$995.00			
	custom finish	$314.50		Gold Elite	$1155.00	**September 1991**	American Std (7)	$849.99
	custom finish/gold parts	$359.00		Walnut Elite	$1295.00		Strat Plus	$999.99
	non-tremolo	$259.50		(6) (7) (8)			Deluxe Strat Plus	$1099.99
	+case $57.50						Strat Ultra	$1499.99
	(1) (2) (3)		**January 1984**	Std tremolo M/N	$699.00		Vintage	$1199.99
				Std tremolo R/W	$729.00		Clapton Signature	$1399.99
July 1968	tremolo	$314.50		Std non-tremolo M/N	$629.00		Malmsteen Signature	$1399.99
	custom finish	$330.00		Vintage	$999.00		Beck Signature	$1299.99
	non-tremolo	$264.50		Elite	$999.00		Cray Signature	$1949.99
	+case $57.50			Gold Elite	$1159.00		H.M. Strat Ultra	$1549.99
	(1) (2) (3) (4)			Walnut Elite	$1299.00		(6)	
				(6) (7) (8)				
May 1969	tremolo	$349.50				**January 1993**	American Std (7)	$869.99
	custom finish	$367.00	**January 1985**	Vintage	$749.00		American Classic	$1499.99
	non-tremolo	$299.50		Elite	$799.00		Strat Plus	$999.99
	+case $62.50			Gold Elite	$899.00		Deluxe Strat Plus	$1099.99
	(1) (3) (4)			Walnut Elite	$999.00		Strat Ultra	$1549.99
				(6) (7)			Vintage (7)	$1299.99
March 1970	tremolo R/W	$367.00					Classic '54	$2099.99
	custom finish R/W	$385.00	**January 1986**	Vintage	$799.00		Classic '60	$2099.99
	tremolo M/N	$385.00		Vintage Plus	$879.00		Clapton Signature	$1499.99
	custom finish M/N	$399.50		(6)			Malmsteen Signature	$1499.99
	non-tremolo R/W	$315.00					Beck Signature	$1399.99
	+case $65.00		**March 1987**	American Std	$589.99		Cray Signature	$1949.99
	(5)			Strat Plus	$699.99		S.R. Vaughan Signature	$1399.99
				Vintage	$849.00		Sambora Signature	$1599.99
March 1974	tremolo R/W	$380.00		(6)			Floyd Rose Classic	$1159.99
	custom finish R/W	$398.00					Set-Neck Stratocaster	$2099.99
	tremolo M/N	$398.00	**October 1987**	American Std	$599.99		Set-Neck Floyd	
	custom finish M/N	$412.00		Strat Plus	$759.99		Rose Strat	$2099.99
	non-tremolo R/W	$328.00		Vintage	$899.99		(6)	
	non-tremolo M/N	$346.00		Mary Kaye Ltd Edition	$1049.99			
	+case $67.00			Clapton Signature	$1199.99			
	(5)			Malmsteen Signature	$1199.99			
				(6)				
September 1976	tremolo R/W	$530.00						
	tremolo M/N	$565.00						
	non-tremolo R/W	$485.00						
	non-tremolo M/N	$520.00						
	+case $65.00							
	(5)							

NOTES:
- **(1)** custom finish: +5%
- **(2)** left-handed: +10%
- **(3)** optional neck width: +5%
- **(4)** maple fretboard: +5%
- **(5)** other prices according to appointments
- **(6)** case included in price
- **(7)** specific price for LH models
- **(8)** special custom finishes: +$75/$100

THE STRATOCASTER IN DETAIL

Players and collectors are aware that numerous details distinguish Stratocasters throughout the years. The purpose of this chapter is to examine in greater depth how the most significant features of this legendary guitar have evolved over the last 40 years. The information provided will help to understand why Stratocasters of different periods do not feel, sound, or look the same, as well as contribute to give useful criteria for dating this instrument.

THE NECK
Shape of the headstock

☐ From 1954 until November 1965, the Stratocaster was fitted with a "small" headstock, otherwise typical of the Fender style with its asymetric design and 6 in-line tuners.

☐ By December 1965, the headstock was significantly enlarged, with a prominent lower extension, and it retained that shape until about September 1981.

☐ By Fall 1981, the small headstock was finally reinstated, albeit with minor variances compared to the original design.

Also worth mentioning :
• the early pegheads – mainly 1954 through 1955 – have smoother edges reflecting a "manual" touch, whilst subsequent models have sharper and cleaner edges showing increased mechanization.
• as a rule, the peghead gets slightly thicker with time and noticeable differences thus appear after 1963, 1967 and 1971.
• the Strat, Walnut Strat and Gold Stratocaster were all fitted with an "atrophied" small headstock, which vainly attempted to reproduce the original design.
• in 1980, a special batch of 25 Stratocasters was released with a "reverse" large headstock, meant to emulate the right-handed Stratocasters used by Jimi Hendrix.

Headstock decals

The Fender logo and its assorted markings are fairly good criteria to quickly spot the period of issue of a Stratocaster, provided they have not been tampered with.

☐ Between 1954 and mid-1964, the main decal on the headstock featured the original Fender logo (a.k.a. "spaghetti logo"), in gold lettering with a thin black outline.

☐ In July 1964, a modern scrip logo first appeared on the Stratocaster but, owing to existing inventory, the old style logo was found until at least October 1964. This newer logo (a.k.a. "transition logo") kept a gold lettering with a thin black outline.

detail from Fender factory blueprint

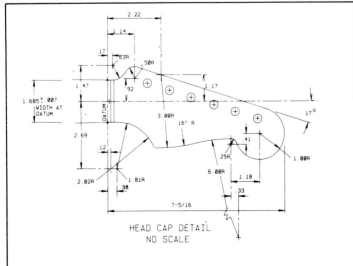

HEAD CAP DETAIL
NO SCALE

☐ In mid-1968, a bolder black logo (a.k.a. "CBS logo") with a thin gold outline was introduced and remained on the regular Stratocaster until about mid-1983. After 1977, the gold outline was slightly increased to the detriment of the black lettering, which then appeared not so bold.

☐ By mid-1983, a downsized silver logo was first used with the advent of the Elite and Standard Stratocasters. This logo (a.k.a. "modern logo" or "silver logo") is still a current feature on the American Standard and the Strat Plus.

Up to 1960, the main decal exclusived mentioned "FENDER STRATOCASTER WITH SYNCHRONIZED TREMOLO", or simply "FENDER STRATOCASTER" on non-tremolo models. After 1960, various patent numbers were added beneath the words "with synchronized tremolo" and they are a safe criterion to assess the originality of the headstock markings on a guitar made between 1961 and 1976.
The changes in patent numbers occurred as follows
• **1961** : 2 patent numbers, i.e.
"PAT 2,573,254 2,741,146"
• **1962** : same 2 numbers, then in Spring 1962, 3 patent numbers, i.e.
"PAT 2,573,254 2,741,146 2,960,900"
• **1963** : same 3 numbers
• **1964** : same 3 numbers, then after mid-1964, 4 patent numbers, i.e.
"PAT 2,573,254 2,741,146 2,960,900 3,143,028"
(NB : the 4 numbers appeared with the "transition logo")
• **1965** : same 4 numbers, then after mid-1965, 5 patent numbers, i.e.
"PAT 2,573,254 2,741,146 2,960.900 3,143,028 2,817,261"
• **1966** : same 5 numbers in January, then only 3 patent numbers, i.e.
"PAT 2,741,146 3,143,028 DES 169,062"
• **1967** : same 3 numbers
• **1968** : same 3 numbers, then after mid-1968, 2 patent numbers, i.e.
"PAT 2,741,146 3,143,028"
(NB : these 2 numbers appeared with the "CBS black logo")
• **1969** : same 2 numbers
• **1970** : same 2 numbers, then ca.mid-1970, only 1 patent number, i.e.
"PAT 2,741,146"
• **1971** : same number
• **1972** : same number, then ca. mid-1972, another patent number, i.e.
"PAT 3,143,028"
This final patent number was kept until 1976 and then disappeared when the serial number was first displayed on the headstock (see PART FOUR "SERIAL NUMBERS").

Also worth mentioning:
• since the introduction of the "CBS black logo" in mid-1968, a small circled "R" (for registered) has always been featured behind FENDER on the headstock decal
• again in 1968, the words "STRATOCASTER" and "WITH SYNCHRONIZED TREMOLO" were significantly enlarged to match the newer Fender logo
• in the course of 1970, the mention "WITH SYNCHRONIZED TREMOLO" was dropped from the headstock
• in 1976, when the serial number was first applied on the headstock, the words "MADE IN USA" were added to the headstock decal. This mention is still a current feature on today's guitars (except those with the old-style logo, such as the Vintage Reissues)
• actually, the CBS black logo was first discarded on the Strat in 1980, as the new model was then fitted with a smaller gold logo with a black outline (cf. the "modern logo", but in gold)
• the Vintage Reissues naturally have the old "spaghetti" logo and they both share a pre-1961 decal, without any patent indication.

When it was introduced, the Stratocaster also featured a small decal reading "ORIGINAL CONTOUR BODY", on the upper bout of the headstock. In 1961, the words "PAT. PEND" were added to the decal, and then replaced by "PATENTED" in 1968. Finally, the whole decal was dropped in 1976, when FENDER started to apply serial numbers on the headstock.

1954

1961

1965

1966

1969

1974

1979 Anniversary

1980 The Strat

1982

1983

1955

1962

mid-1964

1969

1975

1983

FENDER PATENTS

N° **2573254** * (Clarence L. Fender)
filed January 13, 1950
patented October 30, 1951
subject : **"Combination bridge and pick-up assembly for string instruments"**
the drawings featured in the patent show the Broadcaster (Telecaeter) bridge and lead pick-up assembly.

N° **DES 169062** * (Clarence L. Fender)
filed November 21, 1952
patented March 24, 1953
subject : **"... new, original and ornamental design for a guitar..."**
the drawings featured in the patent show the original issue Precision Bass.

N° **2741146** * (Clarence L. Fender)
filed August 30, 1954
patented April 10, 1956
subject : **"Tremolo device for stringed instruments"**
the drawings featured in the patent show the Stratocaster body with its built-in vibrato.

N° **2817261** * (Clarence L. Fender)
filed March 29, 1956
patented December 24, 1957
subject : **"Pick-up and circuit for stringed musical instrument"**
the drawings featured in the patent show a lap steel guitar with a hum cancelling double coil pick up.

N° **2960900** * (Clarence L. Fender)
filed January 13, 1958
patented November 22, 1960
subject : **"... a guitar body having a novel combination of recesses and beveled portions, thereby promoting ease and facility of playing with minimum discomfort to the guitarist..."**
the drawings featured in the patent show a Jazzmaster type guitar body with its contours.

N° **2968204** (Clarence L. Fender)
filed August 13, 1957
patented January 17, 1961
subject : **"Electromagnetic pick-up for lute type musical instrument"**
the drawings featured in the patent show different views of the Fender single coil pick-up.

N° **3143028** * (Clarence L. Fender)
filed August 26, 1963
patented August 4, 1964
subject : **"Adjustable neck construction for guitars and the lire"**
the drawings featured in the patent show different sectional views of a maple neck with a curved rosewood fingerboard and its adjusting truss-rod.

N° **839997** (CBS Inc.)
filed April 28, 1967
registered December 5, 1967
subject : **"Stratocaster trademark for electric guitar. First use in or about 1954 ; in commerce in or about 1954"**
N.B. : Leo Fender did not patent this one !

N° **3550496** (Clarence L. Fender)
patented December 29, 1970
subject : **"Tiltable guitar neck incorporating thrust absorbing pivot and locking element"**
the drawings featured in the patent show different views of the "tilt neck" construction at the body end of the neck.

N° **1058385** (CBS Inc.)
filed June 28, 1976
registered February 8, 1977
subject : **"Strat trademark. First use on or about April 16, 1976 ; in commerce on or about April 16, 1976"**
N.B. : short names also deserve a patent !

(*) These patents were featured at times on the Stratocaster peghead under the words "with synchronized tremolo". However, it is interesting to note they do not always relate directly to the design of the Stratocaster. On the contrary N° 2968204 and 3550496 — as well as N° 839997 — would have deserved a mention.

Fretboard material

A critical feature in terms of sound and looks ! As a rule, a maple fretboard contributes to giving a clearer sound, while rosewood (with the same body and pickups) is probably "meatier".

☐ Between 1954 and mid-1959, the exclusive trim was a fretted one-piece maple neck (Maple Neck hereafter), without any separate fingerboard.

☐ By mid-1959, the guitar was fitted with a rosewood fretboard, milled flat on the neck, hence its current "slab board" nickame.

☐ After July 1962, a "curved" rosewood fretboard (i.e. with a convex base) replaced the "slab" board. At first, the rosewood cap remained fairly thick, but by 1963 it turned into a thinner veneer and it was kept this way until mid-1983.

☐ In May 1967, a maple fretboard became optional and was listed alongside the standard rosewood trim. A glued-on maple board is easily distinguished from a one-pice Maple Neck by the absence of both a walnut spot above the nut and a contrasting stripe (a.k.a. "skunk stripe") on the back of the neck.

☐ In early 1970, the original Maple Neck was reinstated as an option in lieu of the maple board introduced in 1967.

☐ By mid-1983, the curved rosewood fretboard was replaced by a flat cap on the Elite and Standard Stratocaster. This latest variant, which is still the current trim on the American Standard, appeared at the same time as the Biflex truss rod.

Also worth mentioning:
• a bound (rosewood) fretboard was briefly offered on the Stratocaster between 1965 and 1967. Even though it was listed as a standard feature in the 1966-67 catalogue, bound-neck Stratocasters are not abundant.
• although the option was only listed by FENDER in early 1967, earlier "pre-CBS" maple board Stratocasters are known to exist, but they are exceedingly rare!
• in the early 1960's, a few guitars were released with a cocoa bolo fretboard and sometimes FENDER also used hickory instead of maple for its necks.
• the original Maple Neck from the 1950's is sealed with a clear cellulose lacquer (often yellowed with age), but the 1970's and 1980's Maple Necks have a polyester or, more recently, a polyurethane finish (except on the '57 Reissue).
• the Anniversary Stratocaster and the Gold Stratocaster were only available with a one-piece Maple Neck.
• the Walnut Strat was only available with a one-piece Black Walnut neck, but the Walnut Elite was fitted with an ebony fretboard. In the 1960's, ebony fretboards were tried on a few prototypes, but never fitted to production models.
• at the end of the 1970's, FENDER started to systematically install the truss rod from the rear of the neck, no matter the fretboard style. As a consequence, rosewood cap Stratocasters also feature a walnut spot above the nut and a "skunk stripe" on the back of the neck.

Neck radius

☐ Between 1954 and mid-1983, the Stratocaster neck was consistently built with a 7" radius as to offer a slightly convex fretboard.

☐ In 1983, the Elite and Standard Stratocasters were introduced with a flatter 12" neck radius, meant to facilitate string bending.

☐ The American Standard and the Strat Plus have now adopted à 9.5" intermediate size, while the Vintage Reissues share a 7.25" radius.

Position markers

On the Stratocaster, the position markers are made of "dots" located at the 3rd, 5th, 7th, 9th, 12th (double), 15th, 17th, 19th and 21st fret. These dots are useful to date guitars made in the 1960's, in accordance with their size and spacing at the 12th fret.

☐ Between 1954 and mid-1959, the Maple Neck was inlaid with black dots, which, at the 12th fret, almost perfectly cross the A and B strings (= wide spacing).

☐ In mid-1959, the rosewood fretboard received matt whitish dots (a.k.a "clay dots"), which kept the same size and spacing at the 12th fret as the previous black dots.

☐ After mid-1963, the 12th fret dots were moved closer to each other as to become nearly tangential to the A and B strings (= narrow spacing).

NUTS

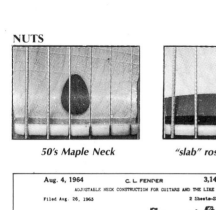

50's Maple Neck   *"slab" rosewood board*   *"curved" rosewood board*   *70's "curved" board with tilt Neck*   *80's "slab" board with Biflex truss rod*

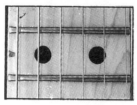

50's black dots   *early "clay dots"*   *"clay dots", 2nd issue*

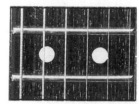

Post mid-60's black dots   *modern whitish dots*   *pearloid dots*

Fender adjustable neck patent

The American Standard and the Strat Plus have an extended 22-fret fingerboard

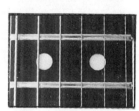

Factory blueprint of the American Standard neck

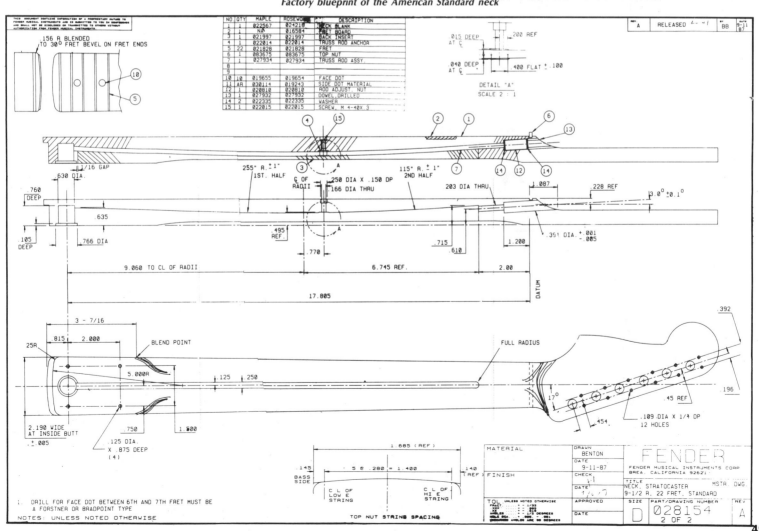

NOTES: UNLESS NOTED OTHERWISE

1. DRILL FOR FACE DOT BETWEEN 6TH AND 7TH FRET MUST BE A FORSTNER OR BRADPOINT TYPE

☐ Ca. February 1965, the clay dots were replaced on the Stratocaster by slightly bigger pearloid dots, which kept the narrow spacing at the 12th fret. These pearloid dots remained a standard appointment on the rosewood fretboard until 1983.

☐ The optional maple board and the Maple Neck re-introduced in 1970 were both fitted with black dots of the same size and spacing as the pearloids dots (i.e. slightly bigger than the 1950's black dots).

☐ Since mid-1983, the pearloid dots have been discontinued and the (slab) rosewood fretboard is now inlaid with white dots, which have kept the narrow spacing at the 12th fret.

Also worth mentioning :
• actually, the recent white dots were first introduced on the '62 Vintage Reissue, as FENDER did not feel like duplicating the original "clay dots".
• likewise, the dots on the Vintage Reissues do not reproduce the correct spacing at the 12th fret of original 1957 and 1962 models. At least, this minor discrepancy can help to distinguish a U.S. Reissue from a Japanese Reissue, because the latter have the correct (original) spacing !
• side dots on the upper edge of the neck also changed over the years. Loosely speaking, they followed the pattern of the fretboard dots, but it should be mentioned that the return of the Maple Neck prompted FENDER to use black (instead of white or pearloid) side dots on the rosewood fretboard models. In the 1960's, the side dots usually sit astride the neck and the fretboard, but during the 1970's, they are often inlaid right into the neck, apart from the fretboard.

Truss rod

☐ Between 1954 and Fall 1971, the Stratocaster was equipped with the classic Fender truss rod, adjustable with a screw located at the body end of the neck, near the rhythm pickup. With this system, the neck is fastened to the body by 4 bolts.

☐ By Fall 1971 the guitar was fitted with the (in)famous "Tilt Neck", which actually incorporates two functions :
– straight truss rod adjustment, with a bullet located above the nut on the headstock,
– neck angle adjustment, with a small wrench inserted in the hole under the bottom screw of the neck plate.
With this system, the neck is fastened by 3 bolts and both neck and body display circular metal plates inside the neck pocket.

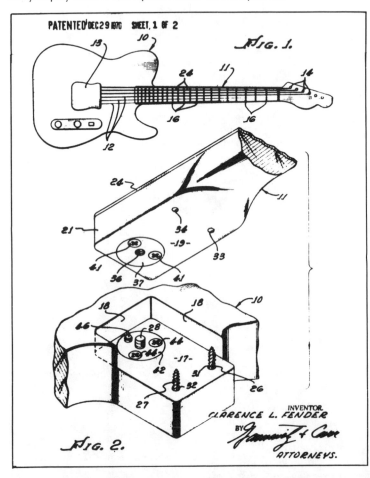

☐ By Fall 1981 the Tilt Neck was discarded on the regular Stratocaster and the classic truss rod was reinstated. In fact, the first model to revert to the old system was the Anniversary Stratocaster in 1979 and later models like the Strat (1980), the Walnut Strat and the Gold Stratocaster (mid-1981) followed suit.

☐ By mid-1983, the Elite and Standard Stratocasters were equipped with the Biflex truss rod, which is basically a much improved Tilt Neck featuring :
– truss rod adjustment in 2 directions (convex and concave), with a nut placed in a well on the headstock,
– neck angle adjustment, with a wrench inserted into the neck plate.
Now, contrary to the Micro Tilt Neck Adjustment, the necks equipped with the Biflex truss rod are fastened with 4 bolts.

Profile

A fairly tricky matter to summarize in words, as the slight variances incurred by the final hand-sanding process makes it uneasy to fully categorize neck profiles according to the years. Besides, it is somewhat difficult to grasp the "feel" of a neck without actually touching it ! Anyway, a few broad guidelines may be of help.

☐ In 1954, the Stratocaster was introduced with a round and clubby neck, with virtually no "V" shape.

☐ By 1955, a "V" spine first appeared and over 1955-1957 "V" necks (a.k.a. "boat necks") were mainly used, albeit with subtle variations.

☐ In the late 1950's, a rounder and flatter pattern was adopted and the neck profile actually became extremely flat in 1959 onwards. In this respect, the earliest rosewood board models are often acknowledged as instruments with some of the best necks ever manufactured by FENDER.

☐ At the time of the L-series numbers a slightly thicker "U" shape gradually appeared and remained in use until about the late 1960's.

☐ By 1969, both flatter or rounder profiles were produced, depending upon the employee and the production schedule. At any rate, variances in the back profile are at their peak during the 1970's !

☐ In late 1981, FENDER purchased a Zuckerman carving machine (made in Austria), which can shape 8 identical necks at a time as per a master model. Therefore, Fender necks have been more consistently shaped since 1982, and their basic trim is a rather flat profile, slightly rounded on the edges.

To further illustrate the evolution of neck profiles in the early days, actual measurements on 1954 through 1965 Stratocasters have been put in table form. These data are excerpted from the FENDER files and were all collected by JOHN PAGE (now production engineer/custom shop coordinator), when he started to work on the Reissues in late 1981.

NECK SPECIFICATIONS

serial number	nut width	thickness at 1st fret	thickness at 12th fret
0193	1.641"	0,912"	1.050"
1111	1.635"	0.900"	0.880"
1023	1.665"	0.920"	0.920"
6586	1.648"	0.912"	0.975"
7978	1.650"	0.885"	0.970"
11987	1.635"	0.900"	0.985"
16731	1.665"	0.900"	1.020"
16874	1.685"	0.940"	1.000"
–18378	1.640"	0.915"	0.982"
–19869	1.628"	0.860"	0.970"
027936	1.655"	0.870"	1.000"
29330	1.640"	0.820"	0.967"
39291	1.660"	0.805"	0.982"
45117	1.640"	0.788"	0.967"
52783	1.655"	0,790"	0.980"
81470	1.645"	0.760"	0.970"
96008	1.660"	0.795"	0.965"
L09542	1.605"	0.850"	1.000"
L10580	1.630"	0.825"	0.985"
L15028	1.645"	0.820"	1.000"
L21449	1.650"	0.800"	0.975"
L44469	1.635"	0.860"	1.000"
L59722	1.640"	0.830"	0.980"
L60083	1.652"	0.830"	0.985"
L86303	1.670"	0.775"	0.980"

Excerpt from the "Tilt Neck" patent filed by Leo Fender in 1970

THE BODY
Wood material

☐ In 1954, the Stratocaster was introduced with an ash body, often figured and generally made of two pieces, although one-piece and three-piece bodies are known to exist.

☐ After 1956, FENDER switched over to alder and ash was then only retained for the guitars with a Blond finish and sometimes custom colours.

☐ In early 1972, the introduction of a "natural" finish prompted the return of ash-bodied Stratocasters. For a period of time, both alder and ash were then used on guitars, but the heavier-density-better-sustain characteristics of ash and its more attractive grain pattern soon gained favour. Therefore alder was practically put aside in the 1970's.

☐ On the threshold of the 1980's, a renewed craze for solid colours, as well as some complaints about the excessive weight of current ash-bodied guitars, put the emphasis once again on alder.

☐ Since FENDER has resumed its manufacturing activities in late 1985, production guitars have an alder body (except the 1987 "limited edition" ash-bodied Vintage Reissues in Blond).

Also worth mentioning :
• As a rule, the 1950's ash-bodied guitars are much lighter than those from the 1970's. Ash is a fairly inconsistent timber and its final density can vary, depending on where it grows.
• Beyond "technical choices", changes in wood may also reflect at times difficulties on the supply side. In the 1950's, wood was real cheap and abundant in whatever quality.
• Outside ash and alder, a few production Stratocasters were made with a mahogany body in the mid-1960's. In 1982, ca. 200 guitars were produced with hackberry wood, which was then used as a substitute for alder.

Contours

The "Comfort Contour Body" is a major feature of the Stratocaster, but not one whose evolution can be easily put into words. By inspecting the front and back contours of a lot of guitars, it is possibile to come up with an overall trend, but exceptions to the rule are not unusual. Discrepancies may occur because of the way both contours-back and top-were actually dressed away at the factory until 1982, namely :
a – a line was traced off of a pattern on the front and back of the square-edged body
b – the body was then laid to an angle and a basic cut was bandsawed, as close as possible to the line
c – the rough contours were then smoothed out on a large belt sander.

The whole contouring process was man-operated and it thus entailed inevitable variances in the above 3 steps. Besides, when the production output was gradually increased to match sales, the employees were left with less time to perform the job. At the end of the day, the contours were pretty much shaped to the operator's discretion. In the 1970's, for instance, some employees did not bother to trace the line and directly bandsawed bodies to cut out contours !

This being said, the following guidelines broadly apply to most guitars and should be used in conjunction with the pictures shown in this book.

☐ As a rule, the 1950's models have deeper contours, and in this respect, the back relief was never as wide as on the 1957-1959 guitars.

☐ On the early 1960's models, the back contour tends to become marginally shorter and on the early CBS Stratocasters it is obviously much shorter (check the back of the upper horn). The top contour follows the same pattern and, for instance, the relief then starts above the level of the strap button, whilst on the 1950's guitars it actually covers more than half of the body bottom edge.

☐ The contours stayed pretty much the same in the late 1960's and early 1970's, but after the mid-1970's they were both drastically reduced as to become quite faint compared to the original 1950's configuration.

☐ More attention was paid to newer models like the Strat or the Gold Stratocaster, but production methods were not modified until late 1981. Modern equipment was then purchased and by 1982 the contours were scooped out on a new machine called an AB shaper, which produces a better and more consistent relief on the back and top of the body.

The current contours on Stratocasters are quite similar to the early 1960's pattern.

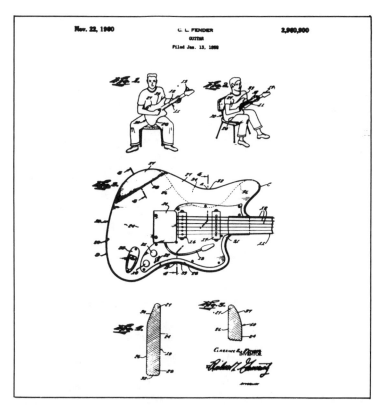

Front page of the patent filed in January 1958 about the "contoured body" and the beveled "off-waist" design (hence the drawing of a Jazzmaster type guitar)

Routings

The inner routings can show some interesting features to assess the originality of an instrument. For instance :

☐ On the 1950's Maple Neck guitars, the control cavity under the pickguard has a vaguely triangular "clean" shape. After mid-1959, a shoulder first appeared in the region of the selector switch and it is a typical feature of the 1960's and 1970's bodies. This shoulder was left to hold one of the 3 additional mounting screws, then used on the new 3-ply pickguard.

☐ Likewise, the number and placement of pickguard screw-holes may be useful to confirm early body dates :
– 1954 to mid-1959, 8 holes only,
– mid-1959 through mid-1983, 11 holes (NB : a very few with 10 holes ca. July 1959), but up to mid-1963 the 2nd top hole from the neck is placed between the front and middle pickup cavities, and then moved closer to the middle pickup after mid-1963,
– in mid-1983, 12 holes on the Standard Stratocaster body, otherwise easy to identify because of its other features,
– the American Standard and the Strat Plus have 11-hole pickguards, but their bodies have a large oblong routing for the 3 pickups.

☐ Between 1954 and ca. 1974, a small channel was routed in the lead p.u. cavity. After the mid-1970's, this cavity became perfectly flat as FENDER slightly increased the depth of the routing to make room for the wires.

☐ On the guitars fitted with a Tilt Neck (late 1971 through late 1981), the neck pocket is slightly modified and shows an additional routing meant for the circular metal plate used with the neck angle adjuster. Besides, the body has only 3 holes (instead of 4) placed in a triangular pattern to house the neck bolts.

☐ After late 1981, the control cavity on the (regular) Stratocaster first showed a small extra recess on the upper edge, where the earth wire was connected.

☐ The body of the Elite and Standard Stratocasters introduced in 1983 cannot be confused with previous models, simply because they do not feature any back routing for the vibrato springs.

The back contour through the years...

1954

1957

1961

1966

1975

1979

1982

1987

Body routing 50's (left) and 60's (right) style. Note shoulder in the controls cavity of the 60's body

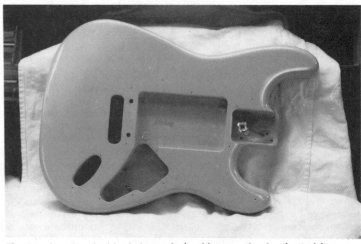

The American Standard body has a single oblong routing for the 3 pickups. Also note the 2 holes for the large pivot posts of the tremolo assembly

The small clamping holes, typical of the 50's and early 60's bodies.
Top left : near the bridge. Bottom left : on the edge of the plug routing.
Top right : near the neck pocket

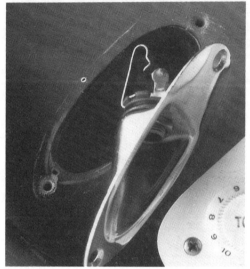

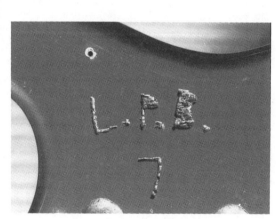

Marking under the pickguard of a 1963 guitar finished in Lake Placid Blue

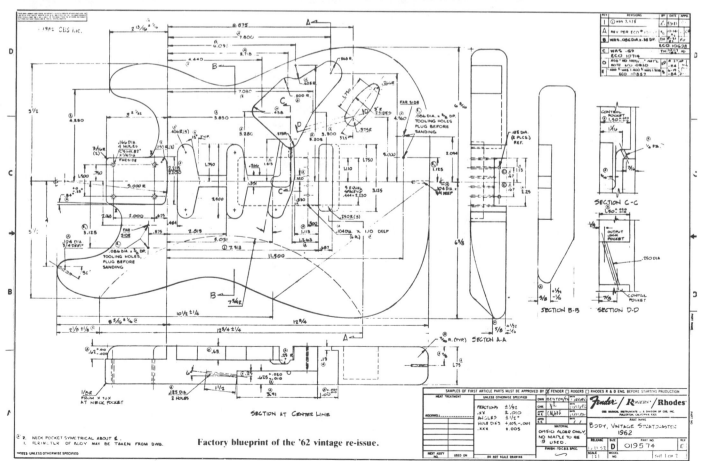

Factory blueprint of the '62 vintage re-issue.

☐ Finally, the small "clamping" holes used until the early 1960's may help to authenticate older bodies and to distinguish them from modern reissues (Fender or else).

The easiest hole to check out is located in the jack plug routing, right above the bigger hole for the lower screw of the receptacle. This hole does not usually appear after 1963. Otherwise, the older bodies also have three other "small holes" worth of interest, respectively placed :

– in the lower horn, within a short distance from the extreme pickguard screw hole (discontinued ca. 1958),

– above the 6 in-line holes drilled for the screws of the bridge base plate, near the pickguard screw hole (discontinued ca. 1963),

– near the neck pocket and the front pickup routing, either slightly above or between both cavities (discontinued ca. 1965).

In the event of an old body being refinished, these small holes are generally filled with paint.

Paints and finishes

A vast subject, which would almost deserve a whole chapter of its own, owing to the numerous finishes used at times by Fender.

☐ When the Stratocaster was introduced in 1954, its only standard finish was a 2-tone dark sunburst shading.

☐ By mid-1958, it was changed for a 3-tone sunburst finish, with red blended in between black and yellow. Until about 1960, however, Fender experienced problems with this new shading, as the red stain kind of faded after it was exposed to daylight. Therefore, many 3-colour guitars look today as if they were originally sprayed with a 2-colour sunburst without any red. Actually, the faulty chemical interaction was pretty unstable and thus some guitars retained the 3-tone shading, while others did not !

☐ The problem was finally solved and after 1960 the model's standard finish became a lasting 3-tone sunburst. Because of its clear separation between the 3 colours, the later sunburst shading cannot be mistaken for the original 1950's finish.

☐ 3-tone sunburst (code-numbered 500 after 1970) remained the "basic" standard finish until its discontinuation in mid-1979.

☐ Meanwhile, the distinction between "standard" and "custom" finishes and its relevant difference in pricing were actually dropped by Fender in 1975. The Stratocaster then became available in a choice of 6 standard finishes at no extra cost, namely Sunburst (500), Blond (501), White (505), Black (506), Natural (521) and Walnut (522).

☐ The notion of custom finishes was reinstated in 1981, at first with the optional "International Colours" (i.e. Morocco Red, Monaco Yellow, etc.) and then with the "Jewel Colours" (i.e. Sapphire Blue, Ruby Red, etc.). But the Stratocaster remained simultaneously available in a choice of several standard finishes, at no extra cost. In late 1981, six standard finishes were first listed (Ref. 521, 530, 531, 532, 580, 506), and then by mid-1983 only 4 (Ref. 531, 532, 549, 506) until the US Standard Stratocaster was discontinued in late 1984.

☐ Since Fender became independent from CBS in 1985, production guitars have been available in a selection of standard finishes (including solid colours), without any differentiation in pricing.

Custom finishes

☐ In the mid-1950's, the primitive notion of custom finish was that Fender would paint a guitar in any available colour upon specific request. In other words, any finish used on a guitar other than its standard finish was deemed a "custom finish". This option first appeared in print at the bottom page of the 1956 catalogue, where it was specified : "STRATOCASTER GUITARS ARE AVAILABLE IN DU-PONT DUCCO COLORS OF THE PLAYER'S CHOICE AT AN ADDITIONAL 5 % COST".

☐ Actually, some custom-coloured Stratocasters were already produced in 1954 and 1955 upon players' request, before the option was officially mentioned in the 1956 catalogue. A few early guitars were also released in Blond, which was then the standard finish on the sister Telecaster, but a custom colour on the Stratocaster. In fact, Blond later became the first "standardized" custom finish with the introduction of the Blond Stratocaster with gold-plated parts in early 1957.

☐ During the 1950's, a handful of Stratocasters were painted with custom colours selected by players, but not by the Fender factory.

Therefore, it is impossible to state with certainty all the colours that were used nor how many custom-painted guitars were released. At any rate, on the basis of the unimpeachable examples in original condition likely to be seen today, early custom-coloured Stratocasters were produced in very limited quantities.

☐ Around late 1957/early 1958, GEORGE FULLERTON came up with the idea of "standardized" custom finishes. In addition to standard finishes certain models would become available in a few optional colours, specially mixed for Fender. Loosely speaking, the rationale was similar to the options offered to their customers by automobile companies. No chart of the available custom finishes was printed in the late 1950's, but it can be gathered from original guitars of the period that, besides Blond, Fiesta Red and Shoreline Gold were among the earliest custom colours retained by Fender. The 1958-59 catalogue, which shows a Fiesta Red Stratocaster with gold-plated parts on the cover, simply specified : "THE STRATOCASTER IS AVAILABLE IN CUSTOM COLORS OR BLOND FINISH AT AN ADDITIONAL 5 % COST". Other colours, such as Black, (Olympic) White, Lake Placid Blue (Metallic) and Sherwood Green (Metallic) were probably used by Fender before 1960, but again custom-coloured Stratocasters are exceedingly rare on the whole until the 1960's. The reason is that solid colours were not terribly popular then, and most players were keener on the more traditional sunburst and blond finishes. Playing a red guitar was certainly considered as the sign of a rebel or at least an eccentric !

☐ Circa 1960, Fender released its first "custom chart", featuring 14 custom finishes displayed in small compressed paint chips. The colours then listed were Lake Placid Blue (metallic), Daphne Blue, Sonic Blue, Shoreline Gold (metallic), Olympic White, Burgundy Mist (metallic), Black, Sherwood Green (metallic), Foam Green, Surf Green, Inca Silver (metallic), Fiesta Red, Dakota Red and Shell Pink. The chart mentioned : "THESE 14 COLORS, PLUS BLOND, AVAILABLE AT 5 % ADDITIONAL COST. SUNBURST FINISH STANDARD AT NO EXTRA COST".

☐ The chart also indicated : "COLORS SUBJECT TO CHANGE WITHOUT NOTICE" and in 1963, Shell Pink was replaced by Candy Apple Red (metallic). This change increased to 6 the number of available metallic colours, which were then quite trendy on cars in general and hot rods in particular. More changes took place in the third chart released in 1965 which, however, still featured 14 solid colours and lasted until 1969.

☐ After 1969, Fender started to delete more custom colours than it added new ones. In the early 1970's the palette of available finishes was drastically reduced from 16 shades down to only 6 in 1974 (including Sunburst and Blond), in acknowledgement of a popular trend in favour of a natural wood appearance.

☐ As indicated previously, the distinction between standard and custom finishes was invalidated in 1975, when the Stratocaster was first offered in 6 "standard" finishes. New shades were added by 1977, but true custom finishes did not reappear until 1981.

☐ The early 1980's witnessed a renewal in the popularity of solid-coloured instruments. In mid-1980, Lake Placid Blue and Candy Apple Red were reintroduced as the standard trim on the Strat, but they were not made optional on the regular model. A few months later, a radically new chart, featuring what was dubbed as the "International Colours" (Ref. 580 through 586), was briefly released in 1981 as a custom option on the last Stratocasters fitted with the Tilt Neck. After the appointment of a new management team at Fender, the "International Colours" were dropped (except Artic White) and replaced by the "Jewel Colours" (Ref. 542 through 548). These colours were temporarily available at a $ 50 additional cost on the Stratocaster, but after mid-1983 most of them became the exclusive attribute of the Elite series until early 1985. In late 1981, Fender also introduced 2-colour "Stratoburst" metallic finishes in 3 styles (bronze, black and blue) for a $ 75 premium. Like the "Jewel Colours", they were mostly used on the Elite series.

☐ Before the Standard Stratocaster was withdrawn from the pricelist in late 1984, 225 guitars were done in a limited edition "Marble" finish (available in Red, Gold and Blue) and shipped in early 1985.

☐ Since late 1985, many custom colours, both old and new, have been used on the Stratocaster and its variants, but they are all available as straight "standard" finishes.

To ease off quick reference, the standard and custom finishes used since 1960 on the (regular) Stratocaster are itemized in chronological charts. A chart indicating the finishes available since 1982 on the Vintage Reissues is also displayed.

Also worth mentioning :

• Black is both the earliest "custom colour" ever used by Fender and the most enduring. It was first shown on the Esquire featured in the 1950 catalogue and, since it first appeared in the 1961 chart, it has been the only finish to be maintained throughout the years !

• Blond (or "Blonde" as it is now spelt) was originally an off-white semi-transparent finish used on furniture. On the earliest Telecasters it usually yellowed with age – hence the nickname "Butterscotch Blond" – because of a very thin clear top coat. The mid-1950's Stratocasters done in Blond still look fairly creamy today, but the finish is much whiter on the late 1950's models and thereafter.

• As a rule, the guitars with the nicest pieces of wood were finished in Blond or in Sunburst and solid colours were generally sprayed on the least attractive bodies. This is why lower range student guitars like the Musicmaster or the Duo Sonic were only available in opaque finishes.

• The Du-pont colours used by Fender were actually automotive paints as American automobile companies always offered a large choice in this respect. Besides, Fender sometimes drew inspiration in the designations adopted by these companies to christen its own finishes. For instance, "Surf Green" was a colour used by General Motors as early as 1955 (Ref. GM111). Late 1950's GM colours, such as "San Marino Blue Metallic" (Ref. GM115) or "Claret Red Metallic" (Ref. GM204) bear a close resemblance to Lake Placid Blue and Burgundy Mist Metallic. This connection may justify certain cosmetic changes in the custom colour chart (e.g. Shoreline Gold vs Firemist Gold) as well as explain – along with ageing – subtle variances in the shade of the "same" referenced paint (have you tried touching up a car's paint with what was purportedly the same finish ?).

• Differences in shades with ageing also depends on the thickness or even the absence of a clear top coat. For instance, some guitars finished in Olympic White during 1960's have turned yellower than others because the colour was not properly sealed with a top coat.

• It is not unusual to find a Sunburst finish sprayed under a solid custom colour. This genuine double finishing originated either in a faulty Sunburst shading or in a hectic production schedule. A few custom-coloured instruments sold in Europe apparently left Fullerton in Sunburst and were painted later in the right colour by the local distributors.

• 1960's bodies sometimes feature markings under the pickguard, either pencilled or crudely etched with a soldering-iron, to designate the finish of the instrument. For instance, "SB" for sunburst, "LPB" for Lake Placid Blue or "FRED" for Fiesta Red.

• Colours other than those mentioned in the charts may be found on perfectly original Stratocasters made after the 1950's. Such finishes were either experimental at plant level, done as a "real" custom job for well-known players, or addressed to a specific export market. For instance, Champagne Gold and Sparkle Red (with flakes), Aqua Marine or Purple (see colour picture of '67 Stratocaster).

• Marble finishes (a.k.a. "bowling ball" finishes) were not sprayed by FENDER in Fullerton, but by a company based in the New York area. Bare bodies were shipped over from California and then returned to FENDER after being "marblized".

• A finished body usually has 3 different kinds of coats: a sealer coat (or undercoat) then a colour coat and finally a cleat top coat. Until about 1968, FENDER mainly used (thin) coats of nitro-cellulose lacquers on its guitars, although some custom colours were actually done with acrylic paints. Nitro-cellulose lacquers are fairly unstable and harder to deal with. So after CBS took over polyester finishes were called in, because they were considered as better suited to mass production. Heavier coats of polyester soon accounted for the change in looks and feel of a guitars as FENDER developed its "Thick-Skin" high-gloss finish in the late 1960's. Bodies were then sprayed with anything like 10-15 coats of polyester! By late 1981, polyurethane replaced polyester for the top coat, and shortly before the close-down of the Fullerton plant it started also to be used for the colour coat. The American Standard has retained the same pattern, with a clear polyester undercoat and polyurethane colour and top coats. Since late 1981, however, Vintage Reissues have been finished with nitro-cellulose all the way up, and like the originals, they also feature a white or light grey sealer coat underneath the finish, depending upon the shade of the colour coat.

• In 1961, FENDER began to dip the bodies of its Sunburst guitars into a bath of "Fullerplast" filler, which accounts for the typical yellow stain found on the wood of most 1960's models. This procedure was dropped with the advent of polyester finishes.

STANDARD STRATOCASTER FINISHES (§)

1960'S CHART	60•61•62•63•64•65•66•67•68•69
Sunburst	
Blond	
Lake Placid Blue	
Daphne Blue	
Blue Ice	
Sonic Blue	
Shoreline Gold	
Firemist Gold	
Olympic White	
Burgundy Mist	
Charcoal Frost	
Black	
Sherwood Green	
Ocean Turquoise	
Foam Green	
Surf Green	
Teal Green	
Inca Silver	
Firemist Silver	
Fiesta Red	
Dakota Red	
Shell Pink	
Candy Apple Red	

1970'S CHART	70•71•72•73•74•75•76•77•78•79
Sunburst (500)	
Blond (501)	
Lake Placid Blue (502)	
Sonic Blue (503)	
Firemist Gold (504)	
[Olympic] White (505)	
Black (506)	
Ocean Turquoise (507)	
Firemist Silver (508)	
Candy Apple Red (509)	
Natural (521)	
Walnut (522)	
Antigua (523)	
Wine (524)	
Tobacco Sunburst (525)	

1980'S CHART	80•81•82•83•84•85•86•87•88•89
[Olympic] White (505)	
Black (506)	
Natural (521)	
Antigua (523)	
Wine (524)	
Tobacco Sunburst (525)	
Cherry Sunburst (530)	
Sienna Sunburst (531)	
Artic White (580)	
Morocco Red (581)	
Monaco Yellow (582)	
Maui Blue (583)	
Capri Orange (584)	
Sahara Taupe (585)	
Cathay Ebony (586)	
Brown Sunburst (532)	
Aztec Gold (542)	
Pewter (543)	
Mocha Brown (544)	
Candy Apple Green (545)	
Emerald Green (546)	
Sapphire Blue (547)	
Ruby Red (548)	
Bronze Stratoburst (550)	
Black Stratoburst (551)	
Blue Stratoburst (552)	
Ivory (549)	
Torino Red (558)	
Gun Metal Blue (568)	

(§) the above charts only apply to the « Standard » Stratocaster and, after 1986, to the American Standard Stratocaster.

VINTAGE REISSUES FINISHES

1980's CHART	80•81•82•83•84•85•86•87•88•89
3-tone Sunburst (500)§	
2-tone Sunburst (503)§	
Lake Placid Blue (502)	
Black (506)	
Candy Apple Red (509)	
Fiesta Red (540)	
Vintage White (541)	
Surf Green (557)	
Blonde (501)§§	

(§) 3-tone Sunburst is available only on the '62 Reissue and 2-tone Sunburst only on the '57 Reissue.

(§§) Blonde was introduced in June 1987 as a "limited edition" finish, coupled with gold parts, on the '57 and '62 Reissues.

THE Fender STRATOCASTER

PICKUPS AND WIRING
Standard pickup assembly

The original configuration is quite straightforward and features :
– 3 identical single coil pickups with 6 staggered Alnico V magnets,
  surrounded by 42 AWG wire windings,
– 1 master volume control (250 K ohm pot),
– 2 tone controls (250 K ohm pots with one .1 MFD capacitor), one each
  for the neck and the middle pickups,
– a 3-position switch selecting either one of the 3 pickups.

This basic assembly and its components underwent only a few visible modifications over the years. For instance :

☐ Around 1970, the capacitor value of the tone controls was first changed from .1 MFD to .05 MFD, in order to achieve a slightly brighter sound.

☐ In late 1974, the staggered pole pieces were replaced by flush poles, as the general use of lighter string gauges made somewhat obsolete the previous set-up.

☐ In 1977, a 5-position switch became factory standard to facilitate selection of the so-called "out-of-phase" two pickup combinations (i.e. neck + mid and mid + bridge pickups).

☐ After mid-1980, a hotter pickup – codenamed X-1 – initially designed for the Strat was fitted in the bridge position on the regular model.

☐ On the Standard Stratocaster introduced in mid-1983, the wiring was modified as to feature only one master tone control. At the same time, the capacitor value was lowered to .022 MFD.

☐ The American Standard released after late 1986 has a revised pickup assembly. The middle pickup is truly out-of-phase to the bridge and neck pickups so as to be in a humbucking mode when the "in-between" positions are selected. In addition to the neck p.u. tone control, the guitar also features a TBX tone control (first devised for the Elite-see below) for the middle and the bridge pickups. The TBX control has a concentric pot 250K ohm audio taper/1000K ohm linear taper and comes with a .82K resistor and a .022 MFD capacitor.

Also worth mentioning :

• In 1954 the staggered height of the pole pieces – i.e. the length of the magnet slugs – ranked as follows : B-E(treble)-G-E(bass)-A and D strings from shortest to tallest. In other words, the D-magnet was taller than the G-magnet, but after 1956, they switched heights and the G-magnet became the tallest.

• Until about 1968 FENDER used waxed cloth conducting wires to connect pickups and controls (white for hot lead and black for ground) and then changed to plastic coated wires.

• Originally, the top and bottom plates of the coil form (= bobbin) were made of black vulcanized fibre. In 1965 the bottom plate became light grey and then dark grey after 1968. By 1980 FENDER started to use one-piece moulded black plastic bobbin.

• Between 1954 and mid-1959 shielding was restricted to a vaguely triangular metal plate under the pickguard, covering the controls and switch area. Upon the introduction of the 3-ply pickguard, FENDER change to a full dimension shielding plate, which stayed in use until around 1968. By 1969 the guitar was again fitted with a smaller metal foil matching the controls area. In late 1981 FENDER reverted to a larger metal foil, glued under the pickguard, so as to cover the pickups and controls area. At any rate, because of its plastic pickup covers shielding was never the Stratocaster's forte, despite mention in early catalogues about "HIGHLY SHIELDED PICKUPS FOR LESS NOISE FROM LIGHTS, SIGNS, etc...".

Of course, beyond these somewhat minor modifications, every player is aware that all of the Stratocasters produced since 1954 do not exactly sound the same, even if they apparently share the same specifications. Actually, the sonic performance of a Stratocaster results from a combination of factors, among which the wood parts (body, neck, fretboard) are not to be disregarded. Each basic component, and not only the pickups, has a subtle influence over sound. Swapping necks (e.g. maple/rosewood) and bodies (e.g. ash/alder), while keeping the same pickup assembly, can easily confirm this point. Now, pickups are often considered to be the crucial components in an electric guitar.

Both the method of construction and the materials used are critical to pickup tone and account for variances in the sound of Stratocasters. In fact, no two pickups are strictly identical in terms of readings and output. A few "not-so-visible" key elements explain why Stratocaster pickups may give different shades in sounds. For instance:

The original (vintage) wiring diagram

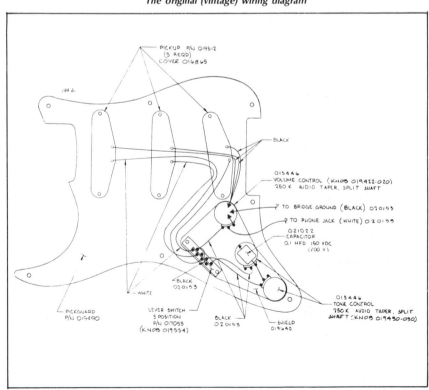

The American Standard wiring diagram

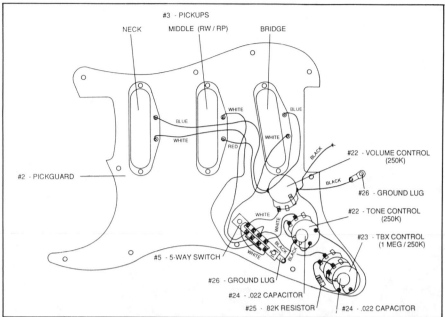

• COIL WIRE
While keeping the same gauge (i.e. 42AWG), FENDER first used formvar wire with a thicker insulation, thus producing a slightly fatter coil. In the early 1960's (dark maroon) plain enamel wire came as an industry replacement and more recently FENDER switched over to polysol (or polycoated) wire, both of them with a thinner insulation.

• MAGNETS
Alnico magnets are made of **AL**uminium, **NI**ckel, **CO**balt plus iron and are available in different grades. The power of the 6 Alnico V magnets found on Stratocaster pickups is subject to variations because of :
   – the ageing process, as magnets lose some power over time
   – the size of the magnets (length & diameter). FENDER used 6 magnets of unequal size between 1954 and late 1974 and even changed their rankings per string during that period. With the advent of flush poles slightly smaller magnets were fitted to the pickups.
   – the actual composition of the magnets. The Alnico V formula calls for specific proportions of metallic elements, but due to the strategic value of Cobalt in the 1950's and 1960's, its nominal share in the formula (20 %) is said to have varied at times.

• WINDING METHOD
In the old days pickups were purportedly "hand wound", that is they were wound on a small belt-driven wrapping machine with an employee engaged in "hand guiding" the wire. The readings for the number of turns came through a belt-driven worm gear counter, which was a fairly inconsistent piece of machinery. This set-up accounted for variances in pickups, due to overlapping wraps of wire or uneven tension inside flared coils. Besides, there was not any "magic" number of turns per coil and, owing to the above winding process, it ranged between ca. 8000 and 8700 windings. This explains why 8350 turns is often cited as the "old" number of windings on early Stratocaster pickups. Finally, testing of wound coils was achieved on a simple volt-ohm meter with a ±20% tolerance, which allowed for substantial variances in the output of the early pickups.

By 1960, the hand-guided wrapping machines were gradually replaced by modern automatic winders. This change in equipment brought about "conversion ratios", i.e. "how many turns on an automatic winder equal the previous average number of turns on a hand-guided machine ?" During the 1960's, FENDER changed back and forth, before settling down for 7600 windings. The main issue was the tension in winding, which can stretch wire and affect its diameter and length, which in turn influence the D.C. resistance (see below). Newer coils are more consistent with neatly parallel winding, but as a rule they are not wrapped as tightly as the older ones, because wrapping tight on an automatic winder tends to break wire. Therefore, older pickups usually have a slightly higher output, while newer ones have a little more top frequency response.

• ENCAPSULATION OF THE COIL
The early pickups were dipped in a hot wax bath in order to solidify the wound coil, but sometimes the wax did not fully penetrate the coil, thus creating a possible source of microphonic noises in the case of loose windings. In the mid-1960's CBS/FENDER apparently made a mistake in ordering wire supplies and was forced to stop dipping pickups in wax as it shorted the coil. Encapsulation of the coil was only resumed after late 1981.

Other pickup assemblies

■ THE STRAT (mid-1980 through mid-1983)
On the Strat the middle pickup tone control was replaced by a twin mode rotary selector, which gives 4 additional sounds, namely :
• neck and middle pickup in series,
• middle and bridge pickups in series,
• neck and bridge pickups in parallel,
• neck and bridge pickups in parallel, with middle pickup in series

The Strat thus delivered 5 + 4 = 9 different basic sounds, in combining the 5-position switch and the twin rotary selector knob. Otherwise, the guitar was fitted with 250K ohm audio taper pots and the master tone control carried a regular .05 MFD capacitor.

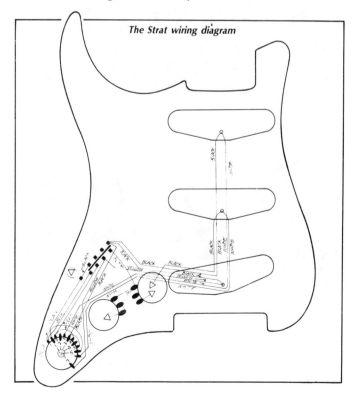

The Strat wiring diagram

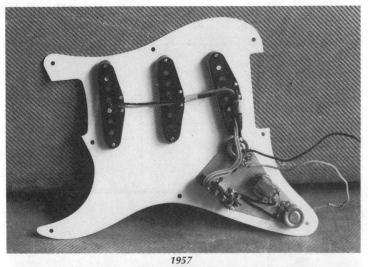

1957

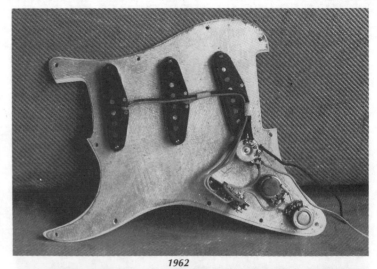

1962

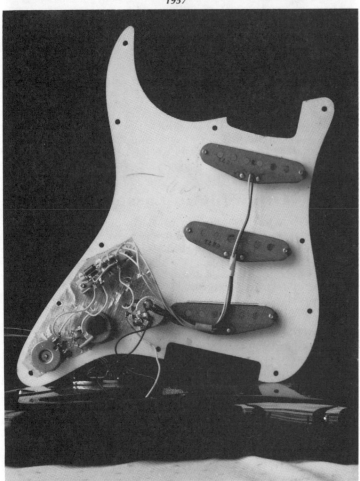

1971

1982

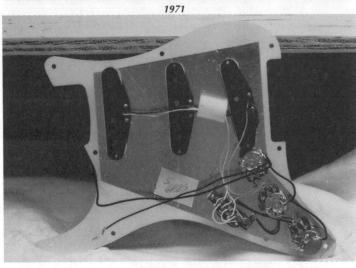

American Standard

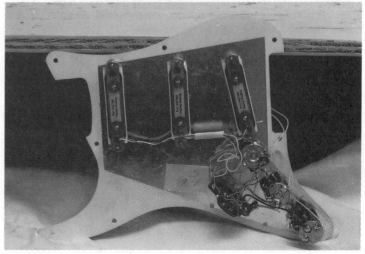

Strat Plus

Mid-50's p.u. with staggered polepieces. Note taller D-string magnet.

Late 60's p.u. with staggered polepieces

Late 70's p.u. with flush polepieces

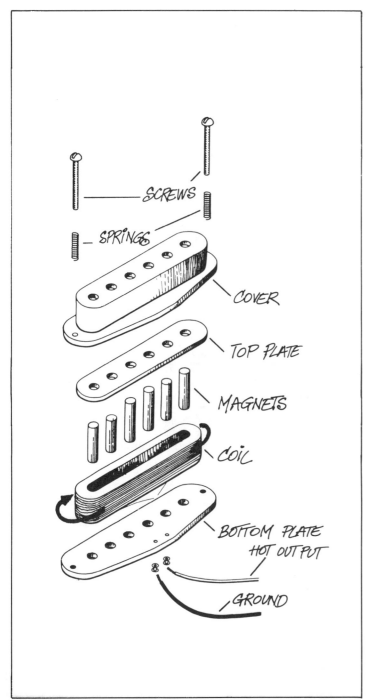

Stratocaster pickup drawing

SCREWS

SPRINGS

COVER

TOP PLATE

MAGNETS

COIL

BOTTOM PLATE
HOT OUTPUT

GROUND

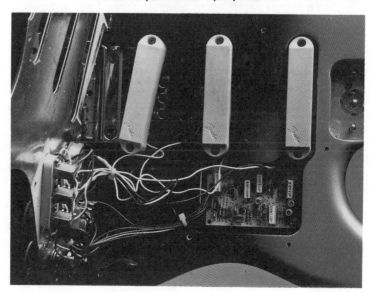

The heart of the Elite Stratocaster

One of the earliest Marauder prototypes was built around a Stratocaster guitar. Note the 4 pickup assembly concealed under the pickguard (courtesy Klaus Blasquiz)

Fender-Lace sensor

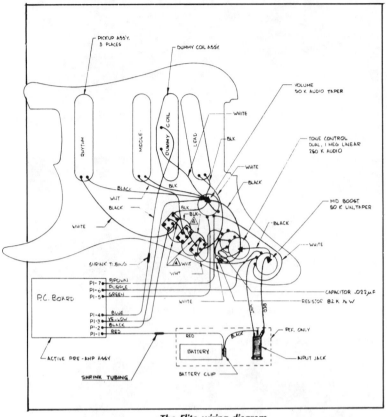

The Elite wiring diagram

■ THE ELITE STRATOCASTER (mid-1983 through early 1985)
The Elite series was a much more ambitious attempt to broaden the tone spectrum of the Stratocaster, as the guitar was equipped with "active" electronics. Whilst a passive tone control can only regulate the amount of treble to be subtracted from the pickup signal, an active tone control can actually modify the frequency response by adding or taking off treble and bass. At the same time, the overall output can also be significantly boosted to make the guitar louder, up to distorsion level.

On the Elite Stratocaster the neck pickup tone control was superseded by a TBX tone control, operating as follows :
• at settings counterclockwise from its mid-point click-stop position, the TBX cuts off high frequencies,
• at settings clockwise from its mid-point click-stop position, the TBX enhances the higher resonant peak of the pickup.

The middle pickup tone control was replaced by the active MDX boost control, which according to its progressive settings enhances the midrange while cutting off high frequencies. To be effective, the controls were supplemented by a P.C. board powered by a 9-volt battery. A dual concentric pot, 250K ohm audio taper/1000K ohm linear taper, was used for the TBX and a 50K ohm linear taper pot for the MDX, while a 50K ohm audio taper pot was fitted on the master volume control.

Because the preamp circuitry can compensate for a reduced output, the pickups were fitted with weaker Alnico II magnets. Quietness of operation was achieved with the addition of a dummy coil, inserted between the middle and the bridge pickup. Finally, the 5-way selector switch was discarded and superseded by 3 separate push/push-on/off switches, allowing any pickup combination. Before the Elite series was discontinued, FENDER modified the circuitry and increased the mid-range boost by a few dB's so that the guitar could emulate the meatier sound of humbucking pickups.

Factory blueprint of the E.C. model pickguard assembly

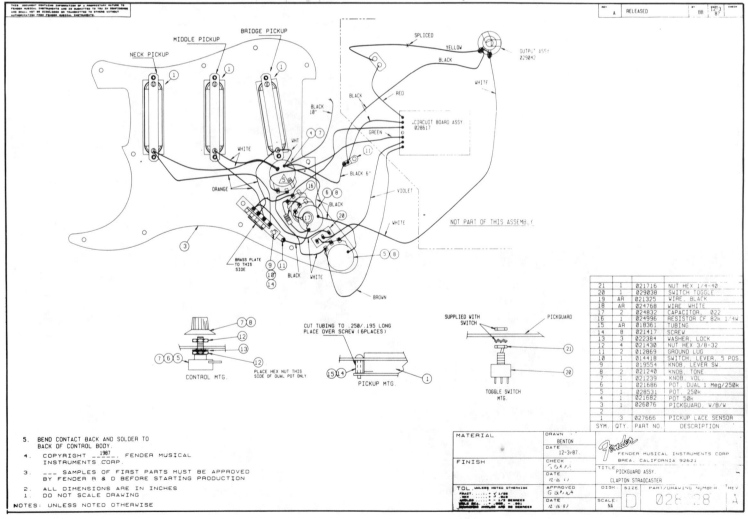

Pickup Specifications

The basic specifications of a number of Stratocaster pickups, past and present, are shown in the accompanying charts. The data come either from factory files, including the information gathered by Dan Smith and John Page while preparing the vintage reissue models, or was specially measured by engineers from the Custom Shop for this author.

Regarding the original single coil units, the charts indicate the average specifications of only two generations of pickup, which loosely speaking refer to the pre-CBS and the CBS eras. But *substantial variations may indeed occur in the measurements of older pickups, even for units of the same vintage.* As a matter of fact, most vintage Stratocasters do not have three pickups that show the same readings. Besides, such measurements may not indicate the actual readings of the pickups when brand new because of the likely effect of the ageing process. Finally, the pickups were all measured on a stand-alone basis with the controls bypassed, and without taking into account the capacitance of a typical cord.

A few words of explanation concerning the main parameters listed in the charts.

* The RESISTANCE per coil (expressed in Ohms) represents the restriction opposed to the flow of electricity because of the wire gauge and length (= number of turns). As a quick rule of thumb, the lower the resistance (all else being equal) the weaker the output and the clearer the tone.

* The INDUCTANCE (expressed in Henries) measures the resistance to alternating currents in relation to the magnetic field. Basically, the higher the inductance, the greater the output but also the greater the loss of high end.

* The TOP FREQUENCY (expressed in Hertz), or resonant peak, shows the higher "natural" frequency of a pickup, and therefore suggests an idea of its timbre. The higher the top frequency, the more trebly is the pickup but the sound is not necessarily cleaner.

* The "Q" FACTOR is supposed to rate the efficiency of a coil and is largely an expression of the ratio of inductance to resistance at a pre-determined frequency (usually 1,000Hz).

The novel FENDER-LACE SENSORS are not electromagnetic pickups but "acoustic emission sensors", namely devices which sense a physically-triggered acoustic emission and translate it into an electronic impulse. The detailed characteristics of the FLS, which are produced by Actodyne General and not directly by Fender, remain classified. In essence, they are passive units built with an intricate array of low energy particle magnets which generate 36 separate magnetic fields "reading" the strings' vibrations. The conventional polepieces are replaced by 36 micro comb teeth whilst the inner core is framed by metal sides that shield the sensors from outside noise and hum. Indeed all the FLS have a phenomenal signal-to-noise ratio compared to traditional single coil pickups.

That said, the sensors perform as pickups and can be measured accordingly. In this respect, it is particularly interesting to note the difference in resistance or top frequency among the various FLS. The measurements confirm not only the versatility of the sensors (single and dual) currently used, but also their ability to be "tailored" to replicate a specific tonal response, eg:

- Gold = late 50s Stratocaster sound
- Silver = punchier Stratocaster sound with more mid-range
- Blue = clean late 50s humbucker sound
- Red = high output humbucker sound

Although it is not strictly speaking a Fender pickup, the DiMarzio humbucker found on the newer Floyd Rose Classic Stratocaster, or the Richie Sambora Signature model, is included in the charts for the sake of comparison.

REGULAR PICKUPS					
DATA	1950s & early 60s	late 60s & 1970s	1980s Standard	Super Strat X-1	Elite
Type of wire	42GA formvar then plain enamel	42GA enamel then polysol	42GA polysol	42GA polysol	42GA polysol
Number of turns	ca. 8,350 in early years then 7,800	7,600	7,800	9,600	9,600
Magnets	Alnico 5	Alnico 5	Alnico 5	Alnico 5	Alnico 2
Resistance (in Ohms)	ca. 6,000	ca. 5,700	6,000	7,500	7,500
Inductance (in Henries)	ca. 2.2	ca. 2.2	2.37	3.27	3.96
"Q" factor	2.2	2.4	2.3	2.7	3.5
Top frequency (in Hertz)	ca. 6,000	ca. 6,400	5,900	6,640	6,640

REGULAR PICKUPS					
DATA	Vintage Reissue	Texas Special neck	Texas Special middle	Texas Special bridge	DiMarzio PAF Pro
Type of wire	42GA plain enamel	43GA polysol	43GA polysol	43GA polysol	n.a.
Number of turns	7,800	8,200	8,500	9,000	n.a.
Magnets	Alnico 5	Alnico 5	Alnico 5	Alnico 5	Alnico 2
Resistance (in Ohms)	6,100	6,210	6,390	6,640	8,100 both coils
Inductance (in Henries)	2.3	2.47	2.50	2.90	4.29
"Q" factor	2.1	2.4	2.4	2.65	2.25
Top frequency (in Hertz)	6,200	n.a.	n.a	n.a.	6,000

FENDER-LACE SENSORS					
DATA	Gold FLS	Silver FLS	Blue FLS	Red FLS	Dual Red	Dual Gold
Resistance (in Ohms)	5,800	7,100	12,800	14,500	29,500	11,250
Inductance (in Henries)	2.40	3.38	6.58	8.12	16.04	4.60
"Q" factor	2.60	2.99	3.23	3.52	3.41	2.57
Top frequency (in Hertz)	4,300	3,300	2,200	2,000	1,700	4,000

HARDWARE
Tuning machines

☐ From 1954 until 1967, the Stratocaster sported nickel-plated (or optional gold-plated) Kluson tuners with an oval metal button and a split shaft. Cosmetically speaking, 3 slightly different types of back cover were used over the period :
• between 1954 and 1957, the cover did not feature any brand stamp,
• between 1957 and 1964, the words "Kluson Deluxe" were stamped in a single line across the cover,
• between 1964 and 1967, the same words were stamped twice in 2 lines across the cover.

☐ In late 1967 the Kluson tuners were dropped and replaced by chrome-plated "Fender keys" (made by Schaller), stamped with a big reverse "F" on the cover.

☐ In 1979, the Anniversary Stratocaster was released with improved keys stamped with "Fender", but made by Sperzel. These tuners did not feature split shafts, but offered string post locking to prevent backlash.

☐ In mid-1980 the Strat was introduced with lubricated Deluxe Schaller keys, also deprived of the split shaft design.

☐ The Vintage Reissues first announced in late 1981 could not be fitted with original tuning machines because the Kluson company had gone out of business. Consequently, FENDER resorted to (good) replicas made by Gotoh in Japan.

☐ By mid-1983 the new Standard Stratocaster finally received improved tuners made by Schaller and the keys in use since 1967 were discarded.

☐ The American Standard is fitted with Deluxe Schaller keys, whilst the Strat Plus has been so far equipped with Sperzel tuners, featuring a string lock system on the back cover. Neither type of machine head has a split shaft.

String guide

☐ Between 1954 and about mid-1956 a round string guide (or string retainer) was screwed on the headstock to hold the top B and E strings on their way from the nut to the tuners.

☐ In 1956 FENDER changed to a "butterfly" clip and by 1959 a small spacer was added underneath.

☐ By late 1971 a second string guide was installed to hold the two middle G and D strings and it became a standard feature on all Stratocasters.

☐ In mid-1983 the Standard and Elite Stratocasters were fitted with two upgraded "Ezy-Glider" string trees, made of a grooved steel rod to allow for a better string vibration.

☐ The same system has been kept on the American Standard, but owing to its Fender/Wilkinson roller nut, the Strat Plus has no string guides on the headstock.

☐ Of course, the Vintage Reissues have been produced with only one string guide since their introduction in late 1981.

Tremolo bridge assembly

☐ From 1954 until about late 1971 the Stratocaster was equipped with the original tremolo-bridge assembly, consisting of :
• a separate inertia bar, made of steel and painted light grey, fixed onto a chrome-plated bridge plate with 3 short, flat-headed Philips screws.
• 6 saddles made of nickel-plated, pressed steel and stamped with the words "FENDER – PAT.PEND".

☐ By 1955 a snap-on chrome-plated cover was added to the bridge.

☐ In late 1971 the original assembly was dropped and replaced by :
• a one-piece die cast tailblock made of chromed Mazac, stamped with the part number (010347) at the string ball end. At the same time, the rear flange of the baseplate was slightly lengthened.
• 6 solid saddles also made of die-cast chromed Mazac, and therefore deprived of any stamp.

☐ In mid-1980 the Strat was introduced with an extra massive brass assembly, and because of the change in material, FENDER reinstated the 2-piece tailblock with a screwed-on inertia bar. A solid resonance bar, stamped with the words "FENDER U.S.A. PAT. PEND", was also added at the rear end of the baseplate to enhance sustain. Improved brass saddles, resting on 12 tracks grooved into the baseplate, completed the new outfit, which was protected by a special epoxy finish (christened formula M52!) to prevent brass discolour. No bridge cover was made available.
The Strat tremolo-bridge assembly was simultaneously offered by FENDER as an optional "Brassmaster Series" accessory. A less massive standard assembly (no resonance bar) was also featured in the same catalogue.

☐ The Vintage Reissues were released with a "vintage style" tremolo bridge assembly, similar to the 1954-1971 outfit, but the saddles are simply stamped twice with "FENDER".

☐ In mid-1983, both the Standard and the Elite Stratocasters were fitted with a redesigned assembly, called the "Freeflyte" tremolo system. On this "third generation" bridge tailpiece, the strings are not loaded from the rear of the body, but dropped in from the top. The new system thus called for the suppression of the classic string-through inertia bar and prompted the advent of asymetric saddles. The knife-edge pivot of the baseplate is no longer directly affixed to the body, but inserted into an adequately grooved metal block, placed under the pickguard and firmly held onto the body by 2 Philips screws. The Freeflyte system also featured a snap-on tremolo arm, but it was not available with a bridge cover.
The Elite Stratocaster was equipped with a more massive assembly, characterized by a solid "resonance" ridge around the baseplate and a reverse "F" stamped at its rear end.

☐ The American Standard assembly (also featured on the Strat Plus) marked the return of a more classic and straightforward tremolo bridge tailpiece. Its thicker bridge baseplate is simply held to the body by 2 long single-slotted screws, so as to create true knife-edge pivots. The separate "string-through" inertia bar is angled to allow for increased downward travel. The redesigned saddles are made of high density "sintered" stainless steel (or "powdered compressed steel"), meant to increase clarity of sound as well as diminish problems caused by worn and rusted plating. This latest assembly comes without a bridge cover.

Pickguard

☐ Between 1954 and mid-1959 the production Stratocasters were fitted with a single ply white pickguard, mounted on the body with 8 Philips screws. The only exceptions to this basic rule are the few guitars released in 1954 and later in 1958 with an anodized gold metal pickguard.

☐ By mid-1959 the rosewood board guitars were equipped with a 3-ply white pickguard (white/black/white), mounted on the body with 11 Philips screws. During a short transition period, ca. July 1959, a few rosewood board Stratocasters were released with hybrid outfits, such as a white single ply pickguard with 8 or even 10 mounting screws, or 3-ply pickguard with only 8 mounting screws !

A white 3-ply pickguard remained the standard appointment of the Stratocaster until 1976, but collectors are fully aware of the valuable details which distinguish the successive variants of the part.
• From mid-1959 up to early 1965 pickguards were made out of celluloid (or Nitrate) material, which even brand new showed a greenish tint. With ageing, the front face usually became even more "greyish" or "greenish" and the pickguard also tended to slightly shrink on the edges.
• After early 1965, celluloid pickguards were discontinued and FENDER then switched over to real white plastic pickguards.
• The earliest 3-ply pickguards (mainly 1959 through 1960) were slightly thinner than later units.
• From mid-1959 until mid-1963 the second upper mounting screw was placed roughly half-way between the neck and the middle pickup cover. After mid-1963 this screw was relocated closer to the middle pickup.

☐ Beginning in 1962 a few Stratocasters were also fitted with a 4-ply pickguard, simulating "tortoise shell", like those found then on the Jazzmaster or the Precision Bass. Shell guards were first made out of celluloid until early 1965, and then out of plastic. They were finally discontinued on the Stratocaster around 1967.

Klusons, 1st style   *Klusons, 2nd style*   *Klusons, 3rd style*   *Fender keys*   *The Strat keys*   *American Std keys*

Original bridge section from the 1950's

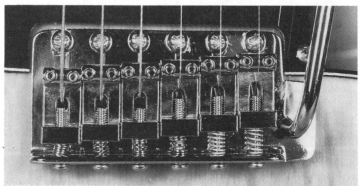

1970's die-cast bridge section

The Elite bridge with "drop-in" string loading

The American Std bridge with its "powdered" steel saddles

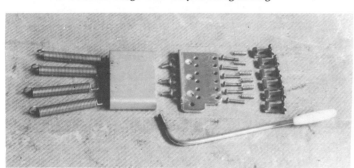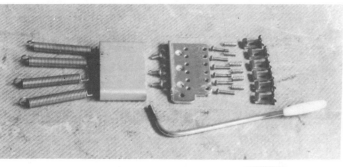

Top : the original vibrato assembly. Left : the Freeflyte tremolo system

Top : 1961 pickguard. Bottom : Late 1963 pickguard. Note the difference in the mounting screws

☐ In 1975 FENDER first released Stratocasters mounted with a 3-ply black pickguard (black/white/black) and by 1976 black became the standard trim on the guitar until late 1980. The only exceptions are the Antigua-finished Stratocasters, The Strat (but not the Walnut Strat) and the Gold Stratocaster.

☐ The 3-ply white pickguard was first reinstated with the new International Custom colours, briefly offered in 1981.

☐ In late 1981 the Vintage Reissues were introduced with replicas of older pickguards, except the '62 model fitted with a 3-ply plastic guard. Besides, FENDER initially misplaced the "upper second screw" and the '62 Reissue first sported a mid-1963 pickguard! This detail was later corrected on production models in 1982.

☐ In mid-1983, the Standard Stratocaster was fitted with a single ply white pickguard, mounted on the body with 12 screws. An extra screw was added near the jack plug, then relocated on the pickguard assembly. Meanwhile, the Elite Stratocaster continued to be offered with a 3-ply white pickguard, mounted with only 11 screws, but the "second" upper screw was moved betwen the neck and middle pickups, like in the early 1960's. The Elite pickguard, however, cannot be mistaken for a vintage piece because it features a slightly different curve in the controls area.

☐ The American Standard and the Strat Plus have both been fitted with 3-ply white plastic pickguards, mounted with 11 screws as per the mid-1963 configuration.

Other parts

☐ The earliest Stratocasters released in 1954 were fitted with unique pearl white knobs and pickup covers. These first knobs were slightly smaller, with a distinct shape which cannot be confused with the standard design introduced a few months later. Likewise, the early pickup covers featured typically rounded edges.

☐ Over the Summer of 1954 FENDER adopted a new mattish white material, known as "Bakelite" among collectors. The new material proved too brittle and it accounts for the small dents usually found on pickup covers as well as extra wear on the knobs.

☐ In late 1955 FENDER started to switch over to more durable white plastic for the knobs and the pickup covers. Slight variances can be detected in the parts used after the mid-1950's, but white plastic was consistently used until 1976, even on the guitars with a metal or a shell pickguard. However, oxydation and ageing can produce different shades of "white", and some parts are more "creamy" or "yellowed" than others.

☐ By 1976 the Standard Stratocaster was offered in an all-black trim and FENDER changed to black knobs (including the tip of the tremolo arm) and pickup covers. Black was continued on small parts until 1981 and was even used on 1981 standard Stratocasters released with a white pickguard (except the Gold Stratocaster).

☐ In mid-1980 The Strat was introduced with brass control knobs, otherwise offered as optional accessories in Fender's Original Brass Works catalogue.

☐ Since late 1981 white knobs and pickup covers have been used throughout. But the Elite Stratocaster was fitted with special knobs, featuring a serrated rubber insert and a backward "F" stamped on top. The Elite also had specific pickup covers, without any holes for the polepieces. Today, the models with Fender-Lace sensors, like the Strat Plus or the Eric Clapton model, also have specific pickup covers.

☐ Otherwise, it should be noted that in mid-1983 the Standard and Elite Stratocasters were factory-equipped with security-lock strap buttons. The same type of buttons, which can still be used with a regular strap, are also fitted to the American Standard and the Strat Plus.

☐ On the first Stratocasters released in 1954, the vibrato backplate was punched with 6 round holes. In early 1955 it was modified to feature 6 bigger oblong holes to facilitate restringing without actually taking off the plate. On the American Standard and the Strat Plus, FENDER has moved one step further and the backplate now has a large rectangular opening for easier access. As a rule, backplates were of the single ply format until the mid-1970's and FENDER first issued 3-ply backplates in 1976 (black/white/black). Today, the American Standard and the Strat Plus are fitted with a 3-ply backplate, matching the pickguard.

American Standard master drawing

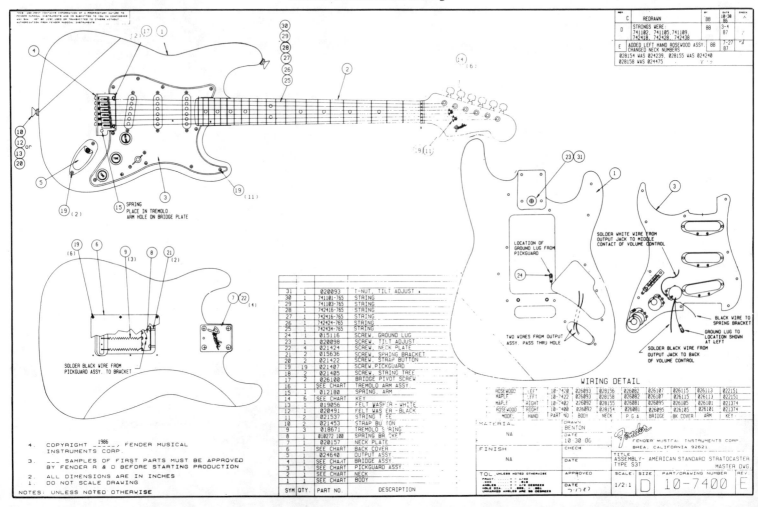

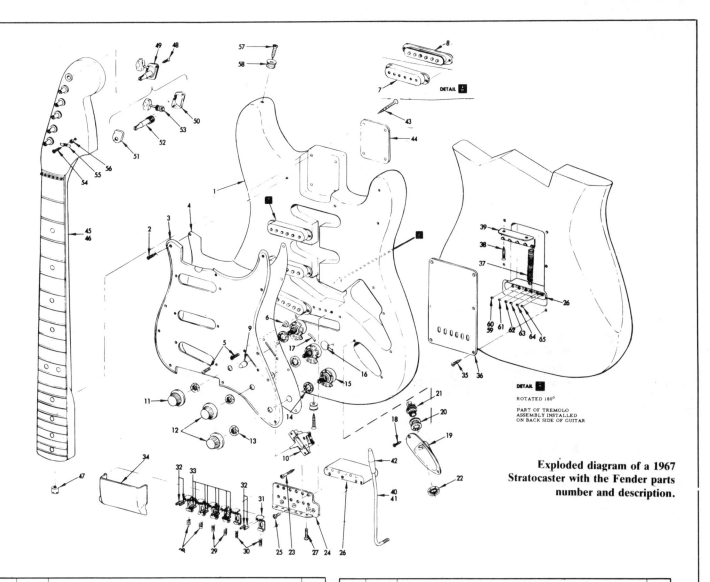

Exploded diagram of a 1967 Stratocaster with the Fender parts number and description.

DETAIL B

ROTATED 180°
PART OF TREMOLO
ASSEMBLY INSTALLED
ON BACK SIDE OF GUITAR

DRAWING KEY NUMBER	PART NUMBER	SUNBURST STRATOCASTER PART DESCRIPTION	QUANITY REQUIRED PER ASSY
		BODY ASSEMBLY	
1	038877	Body - Guitar, Sunburst	1
		PICKGUARD ASSEMBLY	
2	015578	Screw - SM. OV. HD. PHIL. #4 x 1/2 STL. NKL. PLT.	11
3	034843	Pickguard - White	1
4	038935	Shield - Pickguard	1
5	015776	Screw - MACH. OV. HD. PHIL. #6-32 x 9/16STL. NKL.PLT.	8
6	019240	Spring - Compression, Pickup	6
7	016865	Cover - Pickup, White	3
8	038943	Core Assembly - Pickup	3
9	019554	Knob - Lever	1
10	017053	Switch - 3 position	1
11	019430	Knob - Volume	1
12	019422	Knob - Tone	2
13	016352	Nut - Hex 3/8 - 32 THD.	3
14	016436	Washer - Lock, Internal Tooth, 3/8	3
15	035865	Control - Control Volume and Tone 250K	3
16	015537	Capacitor - Ceramic .1 x 50 - 10%	1
17	019091	Sleeving - Class B Yellow	1
		OUTPUT PLUG ASSEMBLY	
18	015578	Screw - SM. OV. HD. PHIL. #4 x 1/2 STL. NKL. PLT	2
19	010280	Plate - Jack, Ferrule	1
20	016436	Washer - Lock Internal Tooth, 3/8	2
21	021956	Jack - Phone, 2 cond. open circuit	1
22	016352	Nut - Hex, 3/8	1
		ADJUSTABLE BRIDGE ASSEMBLY	
23	016170	Screw - WOOD. RD.HD. PHIL. #6 x 1.1/4 STL. NKL. PLT.	6
24	010231	Plate - Bridge Base	1
25	015859	Screws - MACH. FL. HD. PHIL. #8 - 32 x 3/8 STL. NKL. PLT.	3
26	010348	Block - Tremolo	1
27	015693	Screw - MACH. RD. HD. PHIL. #4-40 x 7/8 STL. NKL. PLT.	6
28	019273	Spring - Compression 1/4 Long	2
29	019281	Spring - Compression 5/16 Long	2
30	019364	Spring - Compression 7/16 Long	2
31	027037	Bar - Bridge	6
32	016089	Screw - Set. SOC. OV. PT. #4 - 40 x 5.16STL. NKL. PLT.	4
33	016071	Screw - Set. SOC. OV. PT. #4 - 40 x 3/8 STL. NKL. PLT.	8
34	010223	Cover - Bridge	1
35	015578	Screw - SM. OV. HD. PHIL. #4 x 1/2 STL. NKL. PLT.	6
36	049254	Plate - White	1
37	018671	Spring - Tension, Nickel	5
38	015644	Screw - SM. OV. HD. PHIL. #8 x 2 In. STL. NKL. PLT.	2
39	010272	Holder - Spring, Tremolo Tension	1
40	038927	Lever Assembly, (Cap & Lever)	1
41	010298	Lever - Tremolo	1
42	019463	Knob - Tremolo	1
		NECK AND KEY ASSEMBLY	
43	015636	Screw - SM. OV. PHIL. #8 x 1, 3/4 STL. NKL. PLT.	4
44	010215	Plate - Neck	1

DRAWING KEY NUMBER	PART NUMBER	SUNBURST STRATOCASTER PART DESCRIPTION	QUANITY REQUIRED PER ASSY
		NECK AND KEY ASSEMBLY (continued)	
45	038844	Neck and Key Assembly (Includes neck with keys installed and neck rod adjusting nut).	1
46	035048	Neck Fabrication Assembly (Includes neck and neck rod adjusting nut).	1
47	012252	Nut - Neck Rod Adjusting	1
		KEY ASSEMBLY	
48	016329	Screw - WOOD. RD. HD. PHIL. #3 x 3/8 STL. NKL. PLT.	
49	053694	Key Assembly Complete	
50	033738	Cover - Key Assembly	
51	033761	Housing - Key Assembly	
52	034330	Post and Gear - Key Assembly	
53	034363	Head and Worm - Metal	
		STRING GUIDE ASSEMBLY	
54	016337	Screw - WOOD. RD. HD. PHIL. #3 x 5/8 STL. NKL. PLT.	1
55	010389	Guide - String	1
56	016881	Spacer - String Guide	1
		STRAP BUTTON ASSEMBLY	
57	016188	Screw - WOOD. OV. HD. PHIL. #6 x 1 STL. NKL. PLT.	2
58	012344	Button - Strap	2
		STRING ASSEMBLY	
59	017798	String Set Complete (6 Strings) (1500)	1
60	017806	String "E" String (1) .012 (1501)	1
61	017814	String "B" String (2) .016 (1502)	1
62	017822	String "G" String (3) .026 (1503)	1
63	017830	String "D" String (4) .034 (1504)	1
64	017848	String "A" String (5) .044 (1505)	1
65	017855	String "E" String (6) .052 (1506)	1
		MISCELLANEOUS PARTS NOT ILLUSTRATED	
	017103	Strap - Guitar	1
	018531	Key - Allen .050	1
	045310	Manual - Instruction	1

HOW TO DATE A STRATOCASTER

Determining a guitar's date of issue calls for experience and a sharp eye for detail, especially with an easy-to-take-apart (i.e. easy-to-forge) Fender instrument. However, provided a Stratocaster has not been tampered with, its dating can be quite successfully dealt with. To do so requires to watch for and compound the following elements (in order of priority/efficiency) :

• the actual markings found at times on the neck, the body or the pickups (see below),

• the structural features and the discriminating details described in the previous sections of this book,

• the serial number, which can be of assistance despite the lack of sheer chronology in the Fender serialization schemes.

In case of doubt about the originality of the guitar, a side-by-side comparison with a contemporary model can be of help. Of course, any expertise on the manufacturing "signatures" of Fender throughout the years is definitely useful to crosscheck the above elements.

DATES AND MARKINGS

Everyone and his brother know that Fender instruments are almost built "like a kit", with components that can be easily taken apart to be replaced or serviced. In the early days, about late 1950, certain parts like the neck and the body started to be actually dated at the factory by the employees who had shaped them. When the Stratocaster was first introduced in 1954, dating parts was a standard procedure at FENDER.

Neck dates

With the notable exception of a few months after Spring 1959 and the 1973-1981 period, Stratocaster necks were quite consistently dated at the heel from 1954 onwards. This date is revealed when the neck is removed or at least loosened from the body, so that its bottom end can be examined. Various dating marks have actually been used at the factory over the past decades:

■ From 1954 up until March 1962, the date was simply pencilled and it shows the month and the year of production in figures.
For example : **"11-57" means November 1957**
" 3-62" means March 1962

On the very first Stratocasters, mainly 1954 through early 1955, the initials of the craftsman who shaped the neck were also mentioned ahead of the date.
For example : **"TG-3-54" means Taddeo Gomez, March 1954**

After April 1959, the dating procedure was temporarily suspended for several months and then resumed in early 1960. Rumour has it that FENDER stopped marking any date because someone complained about an obscene message pencilled on the neck of his new guitar! This explains why the latest Maple Neck Stratocasters from the 1950's and the earliest models with a "slab" rosewood fretboard do not feature a neck date, although they usually carry a body date!
For example: **Stratocaster with S/N 37043 (Maple Neck)**
no neck date, but "4-59" in vibrato springs cavity
Stratocaster with S/N 39367 (Rosewood fretboard)
no neck date, but "7-59" in vibrato springs cavity

■ From March 1962 up until about March 1973, the date was no longer pencilled, but rubber-stamped at the body end of the neck. This second type of marking indicates the first 3 letters of the month and the last 2 digits of the year, as well as a specific code for the model it belongs to, plus the neck width.
For example : **"2 JUN 62 B" belongs to a Stratocaster neck ("2")**
made in June 1962
with a standard nut width ("B")

But, it does not mean in any way that this neck was actually made on June 2nd, 1962 !
At the time FENDER changed to a rubber-stamped marking, each model in the line was given a specific neck code, probably in order to improve inventory duties. For instance : "1" for the Jaguar, "2" for the Stratocaster, "3" for the Telecaster and the Esquire, "4" for the Jazzmaster, "5" for the P. Bass, etc...

Now, some of the codes were changed over the years and the Stratocaster went through 3 different codes between March 1962 and March 1973 :

* "2" between March 1962 and November 1965 (small peghead)
* "13" between December 1965 and ca. late 1967 (enlarged peghead + Kluson tuners)
* "22" after 1967 (enlarged peghead + Fender tuners)

The last letter in the rubber-stamped marking indicates the nut width, as per the following code used on all the Fender instruments.
* "A" = 1 1/2" (1,500')
* "B" = 1 5/8" (1,625")
* "C" = 1 3/4" (1,750")
* "D" = 1 7/8" (1,875")

Back in the early 1960's, "B" was the standard size on the Stratocaster neck, while "A", "C" and "D" were optional at an additional cost. Optional nut widths first appeared in the July 1960 pricelist. "A" and "C" necks are fairly rare on Stratocasters and "D" is, to say the least, extremely unusual.

To further illustrate the neck codes used between 1962 and 1973, the full markings of 12 referenced Stratocasters are shown hereunder :

– S/N 88381	2 NOV 62 B
– S/N 97328	2 FEB 63 B
– S/N L26531	2 JAN 64 B
– S/N L90821	2 JUL 65 B
– S/N 173477	13 OCT 66 B
– S/N 197538	13 AUG 67 B
– S/N 251629	22 APR 68 B
– S/N 254083	22 JUN 69 B
– S/N 303280	22 DEC 70 B
– S/N 310582	22 MAY 71 B
– S/N 354521	22 SEP 72 B
– S/N 400055	22 MAR 73 B

Between March 1962 and ca. March 1973, approximately 9 out of 10 Stratocasters necks were thus consistently dated at the factory and the only exceptions were... sheer omissions or some of the left-handed models. Also, in the late 1960's, a fair number of Fender instruments were marked with a smaller "green stamp", which apparently does not clearly indicate the neck date.
For example : **Stratocaster with S/N 267917**
stamped in green with "22 319 99 B"

Although it has not been crosschecked on a large enough sample of guitars, the last group of figures would allegedly indicate the month and the year, whilst the first group and the last letter respectively show (as before) the model code and the nut width. If this reasoning is accurate, "99" would mean September 1969.

■ After ca. March 1973, CBS/FENDER discontinued decipherable markings on the neck, that is markings likely to instantly show the date of manufacture. Then, necks were sometimes left "blank", without any marking, but most of them were stamped with a new factory code, relating to the product number and type.
For example : **Stratocaster with S/N 450592**
with "O901 2823" rubber-stamped on the neck

The first group of figures "0901" indicates that the neck is meant for a rosewood fretboard Stratocaster, finished with a custom colour. The second group of figures may (?) reveal the date of manufacture, but its actual meaning is not known to the author.

Neck markings throughout the years, i.e. pencilled neck dates up until March 1962, ink-stamped neck dates between 1962 and March 1973, post-1973 neck code and 1980's neck date

Above : 1954 body date in vibrato springs cavity. Below : 1957 body date in mid-pickup routing. Right : 1963 body date in vibrato springs cavity

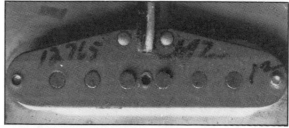

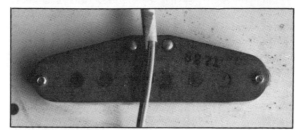

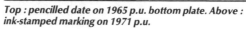

Top : pencilled date on 1965 p.u. bottom plate. Above : ink-stamped marking on 1971 p.u.

Inspection tag on 1982 neck (date : 09 82)

■ After CBS called in a new management team in the course of 1981, clearer marking were finally resumed on the Stratocasters produced at the end of that year. Actually, in order to evidence a more stringent quality control, the first guitars produced after Fall 1981 often show 2 dates on the neck.
For example : **Stratocaster with S/N E207783, rubber-stamped with "9 2 82" under the truss rod adjusting nut and "09 82" on the inspection tag glued under the heel**

In 1983, FENDER adopted a clearer date marking on the necks of the Elite and Standard Stratocasters.
For example : **Elite Stratocaster with S/N E329385 rubber-stamped with "DEC 9 1983"**

As to the Vintage Reissues FENDER logically decided to use a pencilled date marking, showing the exact day of production of the neck.
For example : **'57 Stratocaster Reissue with S/N V002011 pencilled with "1/14/83" i.e. January 14th, 1983**

No guitars were produced in the U.S.A. between February and October 1985, but the same basic dating procedures were reinstated at the Corona plant by the end of 1985.

Body dates

Date marking on the body has not been used by FENDER as consistently as on the neck. Actually, it remained a standard procedure only between 1954 and late 1963 and it was discontinued when custom-coloured instruments began to account for a more substantial share of the production. Like the early neck markings, the body date was pencilled to show the month and the year in figures. Depending upon the years (and also upon the employees who did the job), the body date is located either in the vibrato springs cavity or in the middle pickup routing. As a basic rule of thumb, the body date was at first pencilled in the vibrato springs cavity, then in 1956 it was moved to the mid-pickup routing and finally it was relocated under the vibrato springs in 1959. It should also be mentioned that the neck and body dates of one guitar usually do not match – although it can happen – and in most cases they show a difference of 1 up to 3 months. The following sample of referenced Stratocasters further illustrates these points :

Serial Number	Neck Date	Body Date
0246	4-54	5-54(springs)
12181	6-56	6-56(mid p.u.)
-22759	11-57	10-57(mid p.u.)
026958	6-58	5-58(mid p.u.)
48779	6-60	3-60(springs)
85913	JUN 62	9-62(springs)
L11081	SEP 63	10-63(springs)

The post-1963 Stratocasters no longer feature a regular body date, although a few exceptions are known to exist in the mid-to-late 1970's or in late 1981/early 1982. In such cases, the date pencilled or stamped in the neck pocket does not indicate the day (or month) the body was shaped, but the day it was inspected after being sprayed and buffed.
For example : **non tremolo Stratocaster with S/N S991370 and "11-16-81" marked on the body.**

Owing to its greater availability throughout the years, the neck date is generally considered as the "birthday" of a Fender instrument, and thus players and collectors usually refer to it to log the origin of a Stratocaster. It should be noted, however, that the neck date actually precedes the final assembly of the guitar (and its shipment from the factory) by a few weeks/months. At any rate, it is the most commonly accepted way to date a Stratocaster.

Other markings

Besides the neck and body dates, a Stratocaster can feature at times other markings, likely to help with its dating.

■ For instance, the earliest models produced in 1954 and 1955 usually have a date and a name pencilled on a piece of masking tape, which is affixed in the controls cavity or sometimes on the underside of the pickguard.
For example : **Stratocaster with S/N 0155 has "Gloria 5-26-54" Stratocaster with S/N 0694 has "Virginia 10-28-54" Stratocaster with S/N 6883 has "Mary 9-13-55"**

Such markings show the first name of the employee (always a girl !) who installed the pickup assembly and the very day she did the job at the factory (NB : it wasn't her telephone number !). This procedure was discontinued after 1955, but a date is sometimes mentioned under the pickguard of late 1970's and early 1980's guitars.

Otherwise, the only markings to date a Stratocaster worthy of interest can be found on the bottom plate of the pickups, but they did not appear until 1964.

■ In early 1964 FENDER began to put a date, rubber-stamped with yellow ink, on the bottom plate of its pickups.
For example : **Stratocaster S/N L26531 (neck date : "JAN 64") with "JAN 11, 64" on pickups.**

■ In about January 1965, the black bottom plate was replaced by a light grey one and the date was then hand-written on it, with sometimes the initials of an employee.
For example : **Stratocaster S/N L54382 (neck date : "DEC 64") with "1-15-65" on pickups.**

■ The above markings did not last more than a few years, and by 1969 FENDER started to rubber-stamp a 4 to 6-digit number in black ink on the bottom plate. Although this number sometimes looks like a complete date (i.e. month/day/year), some numbers are "off" and tend to invalidate such a scheme. Nevertheless, after crosschecking several markings, it appears that the last digit(s) indicate the year of production.
For example : **Stratocaster S/N 254083 (neck date : "JUN 69") with "128 9" on pickups (= 1969) Stratocaster S/N 528763 (no neck date) with "1405 74" on pickups (= 1974) Stratocaster S/N S957663 (no neck date) with "1724 78" on pickups (= 1978)**

Such markings may contribute to dating 1970's instruments, which are deprived of any neck date. Mention should be made, however, that one guitar may not have the same code number on its 3 pickups, although they generally share the same indication of year.
For example : **Stratocaster S/N S957663 has "172478" on 2 pickups and "202678" on the 3rd pickup.**

■ In 1980, FENDER began to use one-piece moulded bobbins made of black plastic, which do not feature any markings, except the part reference number "016730".

Finally, a Stratocaster may also feature other markings such as initials, numbers or factory codes on the neck, the body and the pickguard, but they are not of help to determine the age of the guitar.

SERIAL NUMBERS

Although the above markings are the most accurate elements to date a Stratocaster, it is not always possible to reach out for them. Therefore it may be of interest to make some sense out the serial number, in spite of the lack of sheer chronology in the various serialization schemes used by FENDER. Of course, this rationale is valid in as much as the serial number on the guitar is original and that the neck plate, for instance, has not been swapped.

The original series : 1954-1963

■ When the Stratocaster was introduced in 1954, it was at first assigned a serialization scheme of its own, featuring a basic 4-digit number. Based on the oldest neck dates which have surfaced to this day (NB : March 1954) it appears that :
≠ 1 : the Stratocaster series did not actually begin with "0001"
≠ 2 : the earliest numbers were stamped on the vibrato back plate and not on the neck plate.
For example : **S/N 0159 (vibrato plate) with a "3-54" neck date S/N 0193 (vibrato plate) with a "3-54" neck date**

Indeed, lower numbers stamped on the neck plate show later neck dates.
For example : **S/N 0001 (neck plate) with a "6-54" neck date S/N 0080 (neck plate) with a "6-54" neck date.**

Upon close examination, the numbers stamped on the vibrato cover usually reveal a particular feature : the last digit is not perfectly in line with the first three digits and sometimes, it is even slightly set apart. It is dubious to envisage that the Stratocaster was meant to initially sport a 3-digit number, and consequently the only sound explanation is either a faulty stamping machine or a 2-step stamping process. Anyway, numbers in the 0100's and 0200's, stamped on the vibrato back plate, were undoubtedly the earliest (but not the lowest) applied to a Stratocaster.

■ In June 1954 FENDER wisely decided to stamp the serial number on the neck plate, which is more of a structural part on the guitar. Then, straight 4-digit numbers were used up to the early 1200's, albeit without any strict correlation in time.
For example : **S/N 0694 with a "10-54" neck date**
    S/N 0971 with a "8-54" neck date

■ By the end of 1954, FENDER put an end to the 3 parallel numbering schemes of its electric solid bodies (Telecaster, Esquire, P. Bass and Stratocaster) and merged them one series, based on the higher Telecaster rankings. Thus, the Stratocaster suddenly jumped some 5000 numbers ahead.
For example : **S/N 6579 with a "12-54" neck date**
    S/N 6800 with a "1-55" neck date

From then on, numbers progressed within a basic 4 and 5-digit format, growing through 6000's up to 90000's, as they were applied to the whole line of electric guitars and basses. Number 99999 has not been tracked down, but in all logic it was probably used in early 1963.

■ A bunch of 1950's numbers deserve special attention because of the way they were stamped.

• in 1955 and early 1956 some 5-digit numbers beginning with "0" were used instead of straight 4-digit numbers.
For example : **S/N 06823 with a "5-55" neck date**
    S/N 09088 with a "3-56" neck date

• in 1957 and very early 1958 some 5-digit numbers were stamped with a dash in front.
For example : **S/N −17140 with a "3-57" neck date**
    S/N −22770 with a "10-57" neck date

• between late 1957 and mid-1958 some 6-digit numbers beginning with "0" were used instead of straight 5-digit numbers
For example : **S/N 024077 with a "12-57" neck date**
    S/N 026958 with a "6-58" neck date

• between late 1957 and late 1958 some neck plates were double stamped and they have a different number on each side
For example : **S/N 025937 and −25700 with a "10-57" neck date**
    S/N 025178 and −26302 with a "3-58" neck date.

The (visible) 6-digit number is stamped on the outside, while the "minus" number (concealed) is stamped on the underside of the neck plate.

As a rule, serial numbers are stamped on the upper end of the plate, but some numbers were actually stamped on the lower end in the late 1950's and early 1960's.

SERIAL NUMBERS/NECK DATES : 1954 - 1973

S/N	Date	S/N	Date	S/N	Date	S/N	Date	S/N	Date	S/N	Date
0001	6-54	−19208	1-57	55531	3-61	96534	MAY63	L66741	FEB65	204632	SEP67
0012	7-54	−19745	6-57	56099	2-61	97393	MAR63	L68980	MAR65	209645	OCT67
*0146	4-54	−20340	10-57	56101	11-60	97537	APR63	L69431	JAN65	218886	SEP67
*0159	3-54	−20896	8-57	57942	7-60	98045	JAN63	L69806	SEP65	223504	SEP68
*0207	5-54	−21306	9-57	58262	12-60	98891	FEB63	L71021	JAN65	227207	FEB69
0368	6-54	−21633	7-57	58675	5-60	L00201	FEB63	L71815	JUL65	227737	AUG68
0463	7-54	−22486	7-57	59099	2-61	L02227	APR63	L72438	APR65	235464	OCT68
0694	10-54	−22877	10-57	59798	3-61	L04699	OCT63	L74170	MAR65	238853	MAR69
0705	8-54	≠023313] −22984	6-57	61162	7-61	L06531	MAR63	L76385	JUN65	239316	DEC67
0832	11-54			61762	5-61	L09201	SEP63	L77656	APR65	242245	APR68
1095	9-54	≠024302] −25202	1-58	62213	4-61	L10392	NOV63	L78317	JUN65	244389	MAR69
1122	12-54			62691	9-61	L11913	SEP63	L79518	MAR65	249002	MAR68
6579	12-54	025138	12-57	63022	6-61	L12622	JUL63	L81183	OCT65	251629	APR68
6883	9-55	≠025178] −26302	3-58	63124	1-62	L14787	DEC63	L83576	JUN65	254083	JUN69
7164	1-55			64061	6-61	L16993	JAN64	L84748	MAY65	259809	SEP69
7634	12-54	026555	8-58	65344	7-61	L17682	NOV63	L86050	JAN65	263167	JUL69
7774	1-56	026958	6-58	66527	10-61	L19790	OCT63	L86725	MAY65	267777	SEP69
8017	8-55	027282	4-58	66625	8-61	L20222	NOV63	L88924	AUG65	275513	SEP71
8413	12-55	028189	4-58	67222	10-61	L21270	APR64	L90838	NOV65	278927	MAR71
8498	6-55	28836	8-58	68535	11-61	L21506	DEC63	L91997	JUN65	283107	SEP68
8573	11-55	29068	5-58	69687	8-61	L23976	FEB64	L94250	JUL65	296457	NOV70
08999	4-56	29728	9-58	69989	APR62	L25055	MAR64	L95639	JUN65	298330	NOV70
09358	2-56	30108	10-58	70223	11-61	L27985	AUG64	L97757	AUG65	301463	JAN71
09550	5-56	30918	9-58	71642	JUN62	L28717	JAN64	L99159	SEP65	301624	JUL71
09719	10-55	31628	2-59	72149	12-61	L29716	FEB64	L99639	AUG65	304089	DEC70
09913	1-56	31895	12-58	73668	1-62	L30053	JUN64	101244	OCT65	306690	APR71
10041	11-55	32384	2-59	75378	MAY62	L31413	APR64	103681	SEP65	310582	MAY71
10129	2-56	32579	1-59	75812	3-62	L32656	SEP64	105974	JUN65	314571	JUN71
10620	9-55	33135	12-58	76275	2-62	L33385	MAY64	107726	NOV65	323057	MAY71
11251	4-56	33999	1-59	76563	JUL62	L34343	MAY64	112710	NOV65	329921	AUG71
11623	8-56	34617	2-59	78426	OCT62	L37190	AUG64	115068	DEC65	331031	AUG71
12071	5-56	35226	3-59	79200	3-62	L38680	AUG64	116306	JAN66	338002	SEP71
12181	6-56	35440	4-59	79900	APR 62	L41608	SEP64	120131	FEB66	342374	JAN71
12509	10-56	36454	2-59	80745	MAY62	L42575	NOV64	123579	DEC65	354323	SEP72
13070	9-56	36568	3-59	81356	JUL62	L44989	OCT64	125725	FEB66	356137	MAR72
13313	8-56	37798	4-59	82146	SEP62	L45183	OCT64	133465	MAR66	357037	APR72
13771	12-56	38720	9-59	83506	AUG62	L46760	SEP64	138070	FEB66	364067	AUG72
14093	8-56	39252	10-59	84389	JUN62	L48229	NOV64	144884	MAR66	368832	MAY72
14357	11-56	41996	11-59	85977	JUL62	L49993	JUN64	144990	MAY66	368885	JUN72
14405	1-57	42958	11-59	86836	OCT62	L50469	AUG64	152312	APR66	370831	SEP72
15955	6-56	44869	5-60	87983	DEC82	L51927	DEC64	156996	MAR66	371493	JUL72
16355	9-56	45791	2-60	88047	NOV62	L51933	MAR64	160788	JUN66	373353	OCT72
16720	8-57	48217	5-50	89020	OCT62	L53738	DEC64	162979	SEP66	379233	JAN72
16957	12-56	48779	6-60	90745	NOV62	L56419	NOV64	166140	MAY66	380023	NOV71
−17235	5-57	52186	7-60	91954	JAN63	L57791	SEP64	171730	APR66	381409	JAN73
−17416	6-57	52201	10-60	92430	APR63	L58031	DEC64	177190	OCT66	382058	FEB73
−17770	4-57	52815	5-60	93031	JAN63	L62536	APR65	182354	JAN67	382740	DEC72
−18063	7-57	53206	6-60	94418	MAY63	L63181	FEB65	189025	DEC66	390437	AUG72
−18329	4-57	53266	9-60	94563	DEC62	L65546	NOV64	194150	OCT66	400055	MAR73
−18752	2-57			95700	JAN63	L66668	JUL65	197538	AUG67	418357	MAR73

* S/N stamped on vibrato backplate ≠ double-stamped neck plate

The "L" Series: 1963-1965

The "L" series is in all probability the result of a stamping mistake, even though the "Leo's theory" is tempting. When numbers in the 90,000s hit the assembly line, fresh neck plates were stamped but, for some reason, they did not turn out with numbers in the 100,000s but with numbers reading L0001s. In other words, their first digit is not "1" but "L", hence the L-series designation.

The earliest L-numbers – but not necessarily the lowest – appeared on guitars made in late 1962 and they overlapped with the latest numbers from the original series. The bulk of the L-series is, however, found on instruments dating from early 1963 up to mid-1965. A few L-numbers may surface on later guitars with, for instance, an early 1966 neck date, but these are rather exceptions. Otherwise, the L-series ran from L00001 up to L99999 on a roughly cumulative basis, albeit without strict sequential order.

The "F" Series: 1965-1976

When L-numbers in the 90000s came in sight by Spring 1965, CBS/FENDER moved up to 6-digit numbers in the 100,000s but without an "L" prefix. However, the newer plates came up with the typical Fender backward "F" conspicuously stamped below the serial number, hence the "F-series" moniker.

The earliest F-numbers appeared in mid-65, but until the end of the year they overlapped with L-numbers. Owing to a drastically increased production after the mid-60s, F-numbers rapidly moved in thousands and ran from 100,000s up to 700,000s in about 11 years. For the instruments made up to early 1973 (i.e. with numbers up to the low 400,000s), it is possible to work out a tentative dating chart thanks to the available neck dates. The guitars released thereafter (i.e. with numbers from 400,000s up to 700,000s) are more of a problem. The following guidelines, relating to actual shipping dates, were supplied by CBS/Fender several years ago:
- 400,000s numbers: April 1973 through September 1976
- 500,000s numbers: September 1973 through September 1976
- 600,000s numbers: August 1974 through August 1976
- 700,000s numbers: September 1976 through December 1976

Headstock Numbers

In late 1976 Fender ceased to stamp the serial number on the neck plate and began to incorporate it into the headstock decal while a new serialization scheme, meant to indicate the year of the issue, was devised. New-style 7-digit numbers were introduced, with a basic 2-digit prefix showing the year plus 5 digits for the identification of the guitar.

The first prefix briefly used was "76" and the numbers read 76xxxxx with "76" in bolder numerals. But in a matter of months the "76" prefix was discarded and replaced by "S6". This definitely implemented the system still in use today, whereby the first letter shows the decade (S=seventies) and the following numeral the year in the decade (S6 = 1976). Subsequently, the 1980s brought in the E-prefix and the 1990s the N-prefix.

This scheme is clear and simple, but it is not always reliable to date US-made Fender guitars for the following reasons.

  * At the end of each year, new decals reflecting the change in prefix were ordered but the old ones were not instantly discarded, particularly if there were plenty of unused left-overs. As a result, the previous year's decals often continued to be used into the new year. For instance, many guitars actually made in 1980 and 1981 may feature a S9 number.

  * When CBS decided to sell Fender in mid-1984, no "E5" decals were ordered, and until the closedown of the Fullerton plant guitars were shipped with "E4" and even "E3" prefixes. When production was resumed in Corona at the end of 1985, the company had a sizeable inventory of "E4" decals and it took until 1988 to use them up! Thus, E5, E6 and E7 prefixes were never applied to US-made instruments (but they can be found on offshore models). During this period, a few post-CBS instruments meant for export markets were also briefly serialized with an "EE" prefix.

  * In mid-1990 Fender was still using E9 decals when the decision was reached to order nineties decals. The problem is that they did not turn up with "N0" but with "N9" (= 1999!). These wrong decals were used for a time before correct N0 numbers were finally ordered.

These inconsistencies can be easily spotted thanks to the date applied on the neck of the post-1981 instruments.

Other Serial Numbers

Not all the Stratocasters made since the late 70s are fitted with the above-mentioned serial number.

* THE 25TH ANNIVERSARY STRATOCASTER

This model was released with a 6-digit number stamped on the neck plate and beginning with 25. The date of issue is usually determined by the accompanying "certificate of merit".

*THE COLLECTOR'S SERIES

Specific prefixes were assigned to the Gold Stratocaster ("CA") and the Walnut Strat ("CC") made between mid-1981 and early 1983. The earliest Gold Strats also came out with a "CA" prefix before a specific "G0" prefix was adopted.

*THE VINTAGE SERIES

The '57 and '62 US reissues produced since 1982 are fitted with a 7-digit number stamped on the neck plate and beginning with the letter "V". These models feature a neck date but a dating chart would be quite confusing, because the series went back to V000001 when F.M.I. resumed their production in the Corona plant in late 1985.

*THE SIGNATURE SERIES

The full production Signature models are normally fitted with an 8-digit headstock number, meant as an extension of the standard 7-digit numbering scheme. Their serial number is simply prefixed with the letter "S", thereby giving a full prefix reading SN2 for a Signature model made in 1992.

*THE CUSTOM SHOP MODELS

Unless otherwise specified by the customer, the true Custom Shop instruments (i.e. the one-offs) carry normally a 4-digit number assigned on a cumulative basis since late 1987. In other words, the lower the number the older the instrument. This number is applied with a decal on the back of the headstock, but it is often stamped as well on the neck plate. However, not all the Stratocasters made by the Custom Shop are one-offs. The models from the Set-Neck and the American Classic series thus features an 8-digit number prefixed with CN (N=90s).

*THE LIMITED EDITIONS

Models such as the HLE or the 35th Anniversary Stratocaster have a specific serialization showing the rank of each instrument in the batch. For instance: "035 of 500". The more recent Diamond Edition models share the same system, albeit prefixed with DE1 (Harley Davidson Anniversary), DE2 (Playboy Strat), etc.

Summary

For a quick reference, the main serialization schemes used by Fender on production Stratocaster guitars since 1954 are recapped year by year in a global chart. The numbers itemized in this chart apply only to guitars made in the USA and do not encompass offshore instruments. Besides, a rounding exercise means that the various sequences may not fit all of the Stratocasters, even if they should reflect the average year of issue for most of them. For a more precise dating, the neck date may be used, whenever available, to reinforce the vintage suggested by the serial number.

1954 (4 digits)

1957 (with dash)

1958 (6 digits with 0)

1961 (5 digits)

1964 (L. series)

1966 (F. series)

1975 (F. series)

1982 (vintage reissue)

76 + 5 digits (1976)

S7 + 5 digits (ca 1977)

E3 + 5 digits (ca 1983)

*' '54 serial number stamped on the vibrato cover plate.
Note the round holes for the strings typical of the earliest
Stratocaster plates*

BASIC SERIALIZATION SCHEMES
1954-1993

1954	4 digits in the 0100s and 0200s stamped on vibrato plate then 4 digits under 1300s stamped on neck plate
1955	4 or 5 digits (beginning with 0) under 10000s a few 5 digits in the low to mid 10000s
1956	a few 4 or 5 digits (beginning with 0) under 10000s 5 digits in the low to mid 10000s
1957	5 digits in the mid to high 10000s 5 digits in the low 20000s
1958	5 or 6 digits (beginning with 0) in the 20000s 5 digits in the low 30000s
1959	5 digits in the 30000s 5 digits in the low 40000s
1960	5 digits in the 40000s and 50000s
1961	5 digits in the 50000s and 60000s 5 digits in the low 70000s
1962	5 digits in the 60000s, 70000s and 80000s 5 digits in the low 90000s
1963	5 digits in the 80000s and 90000s L+5 digits under 10000s L+5 digits in the 10000s and 20000s
1964	L+5 digits in the 20000s, 30000s, 40000s and 50000s
1965	L+5 digits in the 50000s, 60000s, 70000s, 80000s and 90000s 6 digits in the low 100000s
1966	6 digits in the 100000s and the low 200000s
1967	6 digits in the high 100000s and the low 200000s
1968	6 digits in the mid 200000s
1969	6 digits in the mid to high 200000s a few 6 digits in the low 300000s
1970	6 digits in the high 200000s and low 300000s
1971	6 digits in the low to mid 300000s
1972	6 digits in the 300000s
1973	6 digits in the high 300000s, 400000s and low 500000s
1974	6 digits in the high 400000s, 500000s and low 600000s
1975	6 digits in the high 400000s, 500000s and 600000s
1976	6 digits in the high 500000s, 600000s and low 700000s a few 76+ 5 digits applied with a decal on headstock S6+ 5 digits applied with a decal on headstock
1977	S7 + 5 digits, a few S8+ 5 digits
1978	S8 + 5 digits, a few S7 and S9+ 5 digits
1979	S9 + 5 digits, a few E0+ 5 digits except: 25th Anniversary 25+ 4 digits on neck plate
1980	S9 and E0+ 5 digits, a few E1+ 5 digits except: 25th Anniversary 25+ 4 digits on neck plate
1981	E1+ 5 digits, a few S9 and E0+ 5 digits except: Gold Stratocaster CA+ 5 digits Walnut Strat CC+ 5 digits
1982	E2+ 5 digits, a few E1 and E3+ 5 digits except: Vintage series V+ 6 digits stamped on neck plate Gold Stratocaster CA+ 5 digits Walnut Strat CC+ 5 digits Gold Strat GO+ 5 digits
1983	E3+ 5 digits, a few E2+ 5 digits except: Vintage series V+ 6 digits on neck plate Gold Stratocaster CA+ 5 digits Walnut Strat CC+ 5 digits Gold Strat GO+ 5 digits
1984	E4+ 5 digits, a few E3+ 5 digits except: Vintage series V+ 6 digits on neck plate
1985	E4+ 5 digits, a few E3+ 5 digits except: Vintage series V+ 6 digits on neck plate
1986	E4+ 5 digits except: Vintage series V+ 6 digits on neck plate
1987	E4+ 5 digits except: Vintage series V+ 6 digits on neck plate
1988	E4 and E8+ 5 digits except: Vintage series V+ 6 digits on neck plate Signature series SE8+ 5 digits Custom Shop instruments
1989	E9+ 5 digits, a few E8+ 5 digits except: Vintage series V+ 6 digits on neck plate Signature series SE9+ 5 digits Custom Shop instruments 35th Anniversary 3-digit number of 500
1990	E9 and N0+ 5 digits, a few N9+ 5 digits except: Vintage series V+ 6 digits on neck plate Signature series SN0+ 5 digits Custom Shop instruments 35th Anniversary 3-digit number of 500
1991	N1+ 5 digits, a few N0+ 5 digits except: Vintage series V+ 6 digits on neck plate Signature series SN1+ 5 digits Custom Shop instruments
1992	N2+ 5 digits, a few N1+ 5 digits except: Vintage series V+ 6 digits on neck plate Signature series SN2+ 5 digits Custom Shop instruments
1993	N3+ 5 digits, a few N2+ 5 digits except: Vintage series V+ 6 digits on neck plate Signature series SN3+ 5 digits Custom Shop instruments